CW00866349

A Brief and Practical Guide to EC Law

Second Edition

David Medhurst

Barrister, Temple

OXFORD

BLACKWELL SCIENTIFIC PUBLICATIONS

LONDON EDINBURGH BOSTON

MELBOURNE PARIS BERLIN VIENNA

© David Medhurst 1990, 1994

Blackwell Scientific Publications
Editorial Offices:
Osney Mead, Oxford OX2 0EL
25 John Street, London WC1N 2BL
23 Ainslie Place, Edinburgh EH3 6AJ
238 Main Street, Cambridge,
  Massachusetts 02142, USA
54 University Street, Carlton,
  Victoria 3053, Australia

Other Editorial Offices:
Librairie Arnette SA
1, rue de Lille
75007 Paris
France

Blackwell Wissenschafts-Verlag GmbH
Düsseldorfer Str. 38
D-10707 Berlin
Germany

Blackwell MZV
Feldgasse 13
A-1238 Wien
Austria

First edition published 1990
Second edition published 1994

Set by DP Photosetting, Aylesbury, Bucks
Printed and bound in Great Britain by
Hartnolls Ltd, Bodmin, Cornwall

DISTRIBUTORS

Marston Book Services Ltd
PO Box 87
Oxford OX2 0DT
(*Orders:* Tel: 0865 971155
    Fax: 0865 791927
    Telex: 837515)

USA
Blackwell Scientific Publications, Inc.
238 Main Street
Cambridge, MA 02142
(*Orders:* Tel: 800 759-6102
        617 876 7000)

Canada
Oxford University Press
70 Wynford Drive
Don Mills
Ontario M3C 1J9
(*Orders:* Tel: (416) 441-2941)

Australia
Blackwell Scientific Publications Pty Ltd
54 University Street
Carlton, Victoria 3053
(*Orders:* Tel: 03 347-5552)

British Library
Cataloguing in Publication Data
A catalogue record for this book is
available from the British Library

ISBN 0–632–03432–7

Library of Congress
Cataloging in Publication Data
Medhurst, David.
    A brief and practical guide to EC law /
David Medhurst.—2nd ed.
        p.   cm.
    Includes bibliographical references and
index
    ISBN 0–632–03432–7
    1. Law—European Economic
Community countries—Popular works.
I. Title.
KJE949.M43   1994
349.4—dc20
[344]   93–46402
                              CIP

Contents

Contents

Preface

I have written this book for lawyers who did not study EC law as students and who have since not had the leisure to familiarize themselves with the subject. Few lawyers can have the patience to read the available textbooks. They are too complicated for beginners who are looking for a simple introduction and practical guidance.

I have therefore not tried to say anything grave and weighty, but have endeavoured to write something short and intelligible. To this end I have tried to leave out as much as I dared, rather than cram in as much as I could. I have also written in plain English, explained jargon wherever it appears, and avoided the use of acronyms.

A chapter on how to look up the law and read cases has been included, and there are answers to the questions you dare not ask, such as: 'Where is the European Court?', 'How do I start an action?', 'What is the Advocate General?' 'What kinds of document do I have to prepare?'.

The Union Treaty (Maastricht) has made a new edition of this book essential. The treaty has created a new European Union based upon the old European Economic Community. The latter was not abolished but was simply renamed the European Community and remains as the main component of the new Union. I was tempted to abandon the use of the word Community and write about European Union Law and the EU, but ultimately I decided that it would be better to write, as a rule, 'EC Law' or 'Community Law' as I did in the last edition. I see no reason why the European Union should forget that the Community is its main foundation.

The first eight chapters of this book describe the main treaties, the institutions and the procedure. The rest of the book explains the most important areas of substantive law: free movement, competition, social policy, company law, environmental law and the Common Agricultural Policy. I have not described every proposed new development. That would be too tedious for words, but I have provided enough information to enable the practitioner to understand the significance of new developments as they occur. In short, I have tried to make this book useful.

David Medhurst
January 1994

Acknowledgements

My thanks are due to Robert Spicer for his assistance in the preparation of the index, and to Annabel Wentworth for her assistance in the research for this book.

David Medhurst

Table of Cases

Table of EC Cases

Table of EC Treaties and Conventions

(Page numbers in **bold** type indicate where the text of an article is set out)

Treaties in chronological order:

Table of EC Directives

Table of EC Regulations

Table of EC Commission Decisions

Table of UK Statutes

Table of UK Statutory Instruments

Table of EC Court Rules etc.

Table of English Court Rules

Table of EC Commission Notices

Abbreviations

CAP	Common Agricultural Policy
CCT	Common Customs Tariff
CELEX	Acronym for the Community law database
CMLR	Common Market Law Reports
COREPER	Committee of Permanent Representatives
EAGGF	European Agricultural Guidance and Guarantee Fund
EC	European Community
ECR	European Court Reports
ECSC	European Coal and Steel Community
ECU	European Currency Unit
EEC	European Economic Community
EEIG	European Economic Interest Grouping
EU	European Union
EURATOM	European Atomic Energy Community
EUROVOC	Acronym for a documentary language used by the Publications Office of the European Communities as the basis for a thesaurus for indexing and retrieving information
FEOGA	European Agricultural Guidance and Guarantee Fund (Fonds Europeén d'Orientation et de Garantie Agricole)
JO	Official Journal (Journal Officiel)
JOCE	Official Journal (Journal Officiel des Communautés Europeénnes)
MCA	Monetary Compensatory Amount
OJ	Official Journal
RSC	Rules of the Supreme Court – the procedure rules of the English High Court

Chapter 1

The Treaties

The United Kingdom joined the European Communities on 1 January 1973. To prepare for that event Parliament enacted the European Communities Act on 17 October 1972. In the title to the Act the word Communities is used in the plural because there are three of them: the European Coal and Steel Community (ECSC), the European Atomic Energy Community (Euratom), and the European Community (EC); the latter used to be called the European Economic Community (EEC).

These Communities were created by three European Treaties. The first of these was the ECSC Treaty which was signed in 1951. It was followed by the EEC Treaty and the Euratom Treaty which were both signed in 1957. The 1951 Treaty is commonly known as the Treaty of Paris: the two latter Treaties are known as the Treaties of Rome. The system of law arising out of these Treaties was introduced to the United Kingdom by means of section 2(1) of the European Communities Act, which reads as follows:

'All such rights, powers, liabilities, obligations and restrictions from time to time created or arising by or under the Treaties, and all such remedies and procedures from time to time provided for by or under the Treaties, as in accordance with the Treaties are without further enactment to be given legal effect or used in the United Kingdom shall be recognized and available in law, and be enforced, allowed and followed accordingly.'

The Act does not deliver Community law undiluted to the courts of Britain; it is more subtle than that. Only Community law which is 'without further enactment to be given legal effect' can automatically be used in British courts. Community legislation which confers rights in this way, so that those rights can be used directly in national courts, is said to be directly applicable. There are three main kinds of Community legislation: regulations, the Treaties themselves, and directives. Regulations are usually directly

1

applicable, and Treaty articles can sometimes have direct effect, but directives are not usually directly effective.

Directives are directed to Member States, not individuals, and therefore must be made into British law before they can be used. This process is dealt with by section 2(2) of the Act, which provides for the making of orders in council or regulations by ministers or departments in order to implement Community obligations. Generally Community law finds its way into British law by this process, but sometimes there will be an Act of Parliament which introduces an area of Community law in response to a directive; an example is the Consumer Protection Act 1987.

It used to be thought that a directive never had direct effect, because a directive is, in essence, an order directed to a Member State of the Community, and would appear not to concern the individual at all. But Member States have not always done their duty, and therefore the European Court, by its jurisprudence, has developed a principle that where a Member State does not implement a directive it is nevertheless bound by it as against its citizens.

Having looked at the European Communities Act, and touched upon some of the principles, the next task is to examine the Treaties which form the framework of Community law. The Treaties which were made before Britain joined the Communities are listed in Schedule 1 of the Act but, of course, there are now new Treaties and the old ones have been amended. There is also a welter of annexes, protocols, and declarations. The Office for Official Publications of the European Communities publishes the Treaties in two volumes that are obtainable from Her Majesty's Stationery Office. The most important provisions are set out, very conveniently, in volume 50 of *Halsbury's Statutes* (Butterworths).

Before we begin there are one or two matters to be mentioned which may aid comprehension. When dealing with Community law it is confusing, at first, to be told that there are three treaties and three communities. For practical purposes, however, they have been merged into one, and provisions which occur in one treaty will often be mirrored by parallel provisions in the other two. The combined institution used to be called the European Economic Community or the Common Market. Since 1987 it has officially christened itself the European Community. Europhiles are now calling it the European Union.

On 7 February 1992 the Treaty on European Union, commonly known as the Maastricht Treaty, was signed. It came into force, after all the Member States had ratified it, on 1 November 1993. It has amended the EEC Treaty so as to establish a European Union

founded upon the European Communities; most of the amendments have come into immediate effect. The first amendment to be
made to the EEC Treaty has been to delete the term 'European
Economic Community' and replace it with the term 'European
Community' throughout. The old treaty was given a new name,
and it is now called the Treaty Establishing the European Community, or the EC Treaty; the full text of this new version of the
Treaty is set out in the *Official Journal of the European Communities*
(OJ C224 31.8.92 p1) and also in the *Common Market Law Reports:*
[1992] 1 CMLR 573.

Wherever the word Treaty is used in this book the reader must
take that to mean the EC Treaty, whether in its new or old form as
the context makes plain, unless the sense shows some other treaty
is intended. The new version of the Treaty, with scant exception,
uses the same numbering system as the old; the text is usually the
same as before, but where there are important changes these are
mentioned. In this book all quotations from and references to the
Treaty incorporate the changes brought about by Maastricht.

The ECSC Treaty – The Treaty of Paris

The Treaty Establishing the European Coal and Steel Community
was signed on 18 April 1951 and has been in force since July 1952.
The original signatories were Germany, Belgium, France, Italy,
Luxembourg and the Netherlands. It is an institution which seeks
to direct and control output, markets, supply, and demand in the
limited areas of coal and steel. It served as a model for the EC
Treaty, however, and is a useful introduction to some of the jargon
used in Community law.

After a brief and high-sounding preamble about safeguarding
world peace and resolving age-old rivalries, the ECSC Treaty will
be found to contain some 100 articles divided into four titles.
Article 1 says that the ECSC is founded upon a common market,
without actually defining what this is. Article 3 sets out the goals of
the institutions of this Community. These include ensuring an
orderly supply to the common market, ensuring that consumers
have equal access to sources of production, and the promotion of
international trade.

Article 4 lists those things which are incompatible with this
common market, such as import and export duties, or charges
having equivalent effect, quantitative restrictions on the movement
of products, and state subsidies. The rather awkward phrases

'quantitative restriction' and 'equivalent effect' mean, in broad terms, quotas and taxes discriminating against imported goods. Such terms will be frequently encountered in Community law when the subject under discussion is free movement of goods within the Community.

Title Two of the Treaty is concerned with the institutions of the ECSC. There are five: a High Authority, a Common Assembly, a Special Council of Ministers, a Court of Justice, and a Court of Auditors. The Maastricht Treaty promoted the Court of Auditors to the list of institutions; its task is to audit the accounts of the ECSC. The five institutions have now all been merged with their counterparts in the other two Communities.

Title Three contains various economic and social provisions including a provision in article 65 forbidding agreements tending to distort competition, such as those which fix prices. Title Four contains general and budgetary provisions.

There is a logical structure to the Treaty. First, the objects of the Community are set down: growth of employment, and a rising standard of living. These objects are to be attained by preventing practices which hamper free competition. Then, five institutions are created to carry this policy into effect. Finally, detailed economic and social provisions are made to achieve the aims of the Community. These include rules on prices, competition, production, wages and movement of workers.

The Treaty of Rome

The Treaty Establishing the European Economic Community, commonly known as the Treaty of Rome, was signed at Rome on 25 March 1957. The original signatories were Belgium, Germany, France, Italy, Luxembourg and the Netherlands. This is the Treaty with which one is generally concerned when considering Community law, and in this book it is referred to as the EC Treaty or simply the Treaty. It was amended in some important respects by a treaty called the Single European Act, and has been extensively remodelled by the Maastricht Treaty. In the remodelled Treaty, although the division into parts is rearranged and the titles are renumbered, most of the original numbering system of the articles remains intact but there are some confusions: article 6 is deleted and article 7 becomes article 6; articles 8, 8a, 8b and 8c become respectively articles 7, 7a, 7b and 7c; and there are a few gaps where articles have been deleted altogether. For the most part, however, amendments have been made by adding a letter to an existing paragraph number. The following is a summary of the contents of the Treaty including the amendments wrought by Maastricht:

- There is a preamble to the EC Treaty which speaks of laying the foundations for a closer union among the peoples of Europe, ensuring economic progress by action to eliminate barriers which divide Europe, improving living conditions, and abolishing restrictions on international trade. The preamble, though common lawyers may be tempted to ignore it, contains valuable guidance to the interpretation of the Treaty.
- The Treaty is divided into six parts. Part One, consisting of articles 1 to 7c, deals with general principles. Article 7 states that the common market shall be progressively established during a transitional period of twelve years. The transitional period is often mentioned in the text books; the only important thing to know about it is that it has expired.
- According to article 3 the task of establishing the common market is to be achieved by *inter alia* the elimination, as between Member States, of customs duties and quantitative restrictions on the import and export of goods, a common commercial policy, an internal market characterized by the abolition of obstacles to freedom of movement, a common policy on agriculture and transport, and by ensuring that competition is not distorted. Article 3a was inserted by the Maastricht Treaty; it states that the activities of the Member States are to include the irrevocable fixing of exchange rates so as to lead to the introduction of a single currency, the ECU. Article 4, states that the tasks entrusted to the Community are to be carried out by five institutions:

  - a European Parliament
  - a Council
  - a Commission
  - a Court of Justice
  - a Court of Auditors

  The Court of Auditors is there to audit the accounts of the Community; it used not to feature in the above list but it is made a full institution by the Maastricht Treaty. They are assisted by an Economic and Social Committee. This is a committee of representatives from such bodies as trade unions, employers' associations and consumer groups throughout the Community.
- The European Parliament used to be called the European Assembly but it was renamed by the Single European Act in 1986.

- Part Two, headed 'Citizenship of the Union', articles 8 to 8e, is a new addition made by the Maastricht Treaty. Under article 8 every person holding the nationality of a Member State becomes a citizen of the Union. Citizens have, on matters of administration, the right to petition the European Parliament, and the right to apply to an Ombudsman established by article 138e of the Treaty.
- Part Three of the Treaty, articles 9 to 130y, deals with Community policies. Title I, articles 9 to 37, is concerned with free movement of goods. The first few articles dealing with the elimination of customs duties are now of little interest, as actual customs barriers have been eliminated. Of far more enduring interest are disguised methods for restricting imports, such as special labelling or packaging requirements imposed on imported goods. Such conduct is forbidden by article 30, which states that quantitative restrictions and all measures having equivalent effect are prohibited between Member States.
- Title II of the third part of the Treaty is concerned with the common agricultural policy. Mercifully, no changes are made to this part of the Treaty.
- Title III deals with free movement. Article 48 establishes the right of freedom of movement for workers in the Community. Article 52 deals with the right of establishment of nationals of Member States within the territory of another Member State. This area is becoming increasingly important. Of great interest to companies is article 58 which treats companies in the same way as natural persons for the purposes of freedom of establishment. Article 59 is concerned with freedom to provide services.
- Articles 67 to 73 provided for the gradual abolition of restrictions on movement of capital. From 1 January 1994 the whole of articles 67 to 73 have been replaced by new articles 73b to 73g, which, subject to some limitations, abolish all restrictions on the free movement of capital.
- Title IV deals with transport; article 74 provides for matters within this Title to be governed by a common transport policy. Minor changes are made by the Maastricht Treaty.
- Title V contains article 85, which prohibits as incompatible with the common market agreements which restrict or distort competition within the Community, and article 86, which forbids the abuse by an undertaking of a dominant position within the common market; these are the two provisions most likely to be mentioned whenever there is a problem in competition law. Article 91 is concerned with prevention of dumping and article

92 with state aid to industry. Some changes are made by Maastricht in the area of state aid.

- Title VI is to do with economic and monetary policy; it contains many new additions introduced by the Maastricht Treaty. Articles 105 to 109d contain provisions defining the tasks and powers of the European Central Bank (ECB) and the European System of Central Banks (ESCB) which are established by article 4a of the Treaty.
- Title VII deals with the common commercial policy of the Community. Minor changes are made by Maastricht.
- Title VIII is concerned with social policy. Its provisions, which have been hardly altered by Maastricht, have proved useful to English lawyers because English law lags behind Community law in this area, and Community law has provided remedies where English law provided none. Under article 117 Member States agree upon the need to promote improved working conditions and an improved standard of living for workers. Article 119 provides for the application of the principle that men and women should receive equal pay for equal work. Because, at Maastricht, the United Kingdom refused to agree to any changes to this part of the Treaty, the other Member States made an agreement to use the machinery of the Community in order to take measures to implement among themselves the policy set out in the European Social Charter; this is explained in more detail in Chapter 14 of this book.
- Titles IX to XVII are recent additions, made by the Single European Act and expanded by the Maastricht Treaty, dealing with culture, public health, consumer protection, trans–European networks (for transport, telecommunications, and energy), industry, economic and social cohesion, research and technological development, the environment, and development cooperation.
- Part Four concerns Member States agreeing to associate certain non-European countries with the Community. It is of political rather than legal interest.
- Part Five deals with the institutions of the Community, making detailed provisions in articles 137 to 192 for the powers and constitution of the European Parliament, Council of Ministers, Commission, Court of Justice, and Court of Auditors. Amendments have been made to this part of the Treaty to increase the power of Parliament.
- Article 189 sets out the various subsidiary forms of legislation used by the Community which are: regulations, directives, and decisions.

Although it is by no means an exact analogy, the Treaty can be considered as a kind of constitution. Regulations and directives are rather like our acts of Parliament. Regulations are directly applicable in all Member States. Directives are binding only as to the results to be achieved, and thus require legislation in Member States before they can come into effect. An essential feature to grasp about the EC Treaty is that it establishes four freedoms: the right to free movement of goods, persons, services, and capital. It also establishes common policies for agriculture, fisheries, transport, and commerce.

Protocols

There are several protocols attached to the Treaty of Rome. The most important of these, to lawyers, is the Protocol on the Statute of the Court of Justice of the European Economic Community. It is necessary to refer to this Statute in order to understand how the European Court operates. Title III of the Statute contains the basic procedural provisions for the Court.

The Euratom Treaty

The Treaty Establishing the European Atomic Energy Community was signed at Rome on 25 March 1957. The original signatories were Belgium, Germany, France, Italy, Luxembourg and the Netherlands. The task of this Community is to contribute towards the raising of standards of living in Member States by creating the conditions necessary to the establishment and growth of nuclear industries. The architecture of the Euratom Treaty is similar to that of the Treaties which establish the other two communities. Articles 92 to 106 set up a Nuclear Common Market.

The Merger Treaty and the Convention on Common Institutions

The foregoing Treaties having been made, it became clear that a tidying up operation was needed. There were three Communities, but each had its own institutions. The Convention on Certain Institutions Common to the European Communities was signed on 25 March 1957. Its effect was to merge the Assembly (now the European Parliament), the Court of Justice, and the Economic and

Social Committee of the various communities. The Treaty Establishing a Single Council and a Single Commission of the European Communities was signed at Brussels on 8 April 1965 and came into force on 1 July 1967.

The First Accession Treaty

The Treaty Concerning the Accession of the Kingdom of Denmark, Ireland, the Kingdom of Norway and the United Kingdom of Great Britain and Northern Ireland was signed on 22 January 1972. Norway backed out at the last moment. The United Kingdom deposited an instrument of ratification on 18 October 1972 and the Treaty entered into force, for the United Kingdom, on 1 January 1973.

From the date of accession the provisions of the original Treaties and the acts adopted by the institutions were made binding on the new Member States. There were various transitional provisions in the Treaty but the transitional period has now past. For most purposes the law can be read as if the United Kingdom had belonged to the Community from its inception.

Gibraltar, the Channel Isles, Cyprus, Isle of Man

The EC Treaty, by virtue of article 227(4), applies to those European territories for whose external relations a Member State is responsible. Gibraltar is thus a part of the European Community, although it is not subject to the Community rules on the Common Agricultural Policy and value added tax. By contrast, the sovereign base area of Cyprus does not come within the Community at all.

The Channel Islands and the Isle of Man have managed to have their cake and eat it. Their anomalous position is covered by the Third Protocol to the First Accession Treaty. Under the provisions of this protocol only the Community rules on free movement of goods apply. Conversely, Manxmen and Channel Islanders do not benefit from the Community rules on free movement of persons. The latter restriction can be circumvented by being ordinarily resident in the United Kingdom for five years.

The Second Accession Treaty

The Treaty Concerning the Accession of the Hellenic Republic was signed in Athens on 28 May 1979 and came into effect on 1 January

1981. Detailed transitional provisions are set out in the Treaty, most of which deal with agriculture, an area of major importance in the Greek economy. The Community provisions on free movement of workers did not come into effect until 1 January 1988.

The Third Accession Treaty

The Treaty Concerning the Accession of the Kingdom of Spain and the Portuguese Republic was signed in Lisbon and Madrid on 12 January 1985 and came into effect on 1 January 1986. Detailed transitional provisions are set out in the Treaty, but most of these interim arrangements were spent by January 1993 and Spanish and Portuguese workers have full free movement rights within the Community.

The Single European Act

The Single European Act is a treaty that was signed in Luxembourg on 17 February 1986, and at the Hague on 28 February 1986. It came into force on 1 July 1987. It made extensive amendments to the other basic Community legislation and therefore should not be discussed in isolation. The full text can be found in the *Common Market Law Reports*: [1987] 2 CMLR 741.

The philosophy behind the Single Act, to initiate a change in relations between the European States into a European Union, is contained in the first paragraph of the preamble. To this end article 2 created a European Council to bring together the Heads of Government of the European Communities at least twice a year. This merely formalized the regular meetings which were already taking place.

A number of amendments to the EC Treaty dealt with the machinery of Community institutions. A co-operation procedure was established, which gave the European Parliament rather greater influence over the legislative process. This procedure is now to be found in article 189c of the EC Treaty; it is complicated. Parliament can table amendments to legislation proposed by the Commission upon which the Council has adopted a common position. If Parliament rejects that common position the Council can adopt the act only by unanimity; in other words the Council can ignore Parliament if it wishes.

Of practical interest to lawyers is an amendment of the EC Treaty which created a new Court of First Instance attached to the European Court. It has jurisdiction to hear certain kinds of cases, subject to a right of appeal on points of law only. At first it was concerned with competition cases and the internal staff cases of the Community, but in 1993 its jurisdiction was extended to include cases brought by natural and legal persons, that is to say private litigants. It is fondly hoped that the new court will reduce delays.

Those articles now to be found in the EC Treaty that deal with economic and social cohesion, research and technological development, and the environment are the result of the Single European Act.

The prime object of the Single European Act was to provide an accelerated programme for the creation of the internal market, described in article 7a (formerly 8a) of the EC Treaty as an area without internal frontiers in which the free movement of goods, persons, services and capital is ensured. A Commission White Paper of June 1985 on Completing the Internal Market, obtainable from HMSO: ISBN 92–825–5436–8, described the obstacles hindering the internal market, and the programme of legislation involved. For example, in the area of public procurement, governments tended to be nationalistic in the way in which they awarded large public contracts. The White Paper proposed more transparency; that is to say, that such contracts should be open to Community–wide competition.

At the time that the White Paper was written legislation already existed, in the shape of directives requiring large contracts for public works and public supplies to be subject to fair procedures for tendering, but the directives were largely ignored. Legislation was therefore introduced to enforce compliance with these directives, and to extend their effect to water, energy, transport and telecommunications undertakings. Another example of an obstacle to free movement was the absence of legislation recognizing the equivalence of professional qualifications. New legislation was introduced to make job relocation easier. The present state of this legislation is described in Chapters 9 and 11 of this book. The target date for the creation of the internal market was 31 December 1992 and by that date most of the legislation proposed in the 1985 White Paper had been brought into effect.

The Maastricht Treaty

The Treaty on European Union was agreed on 11 December 1991 by the European leaders meeting at Maastricht. The treaty was signed on 7 February 1992 and was to come into effect on 1 January 1993, or as soon thereafter as it was ratified by all the Member States, an event that did not take place until 1 November 1993. The full text can be found in the *Common Market Law Reports*: [1992] 1 CMLR 719, and in the *Official Journal of the European Communities*: (OJ C224 31.8.92 p1). It is commonly called the Maastricht Treaty, but properly should be called the Union Treaty.

By this treaty the twelve Member States of the Community resolved to form a European Union, which bureaucrats now call the EU, founded on the existing European Communities. The Treaty of Rome was therefore altered, stitched, patched and renamed the Treaty Establishing the European Community. The new European Community which will be created by these amendments forms the first pillar of the Union.

The second pillar of the Union is a common foreign and security policy; its provisions are set out in Title V of the Union Treaty. It stands outside the scope of the existing treaties and it is based on inter–governmental co–operation.

The third pillar, also based on inter–governmental co-operation, is set out in Title VI of the Union Treaty, and consists of provisions on justice and home affairs. A prime concern is to create a common policy on asylum. Other areas of common interest include judicial cooperation in criminal matters, international fraud and drug trafficking.

The signatories, in the preamble to the Union Treaty, declare, amongst other fine hopes too tedious to recount, that they have resolved to establish an economic and monetary union with a single currency, and a citizenship common to nationals of their countries; and, resolved that the onward march of this Leviathan will be tempered by subsidiarity, they decide to establish a European Union.

The Union Treaty is divided into seven titles. Title I contains common provisions. Article A establishes the new European Union. Article B sets out a list of the objectives of this Union, including the promotion of sustainable economic progress, the protection of the rights of nationals through the introduction of a citizenship of the Union, the development of close cooperation on justice and home affairs, and the maintenance of the *acquis Communautaire*; the latter is nowhere defined, but means the established law and practice of the Community.

Title II contains provisions amending the Treaty Establishing the European Economic Community with a view to establishing the

European Community; in other words, this is the part of the treaty which stitches and patches the old EC Treaty. Articles 2 and 3 of the EC Treaty are entirely replaced. These articles contained the list of purposes and activities of the Community. There is now a much longer and more comprehensive list. A new article 3b endeavours to define subsidiarity; it is not improved by paraphrase, so here it is in full:

> *Article 3b.* The Community shall act within the limits of the powers conferred upon it by this Treaty and of the objectives assigned to it therein.
>
> In areas which do not fall within its exclusive competence, the Community shall take action, in accordance with the principle of subsidiarity, only if and so far as the objectives of the proposed action cannot be sufficiently achieved by the Member States and can therefore, by reason of the scale or effects of the proposed action, be better achieved by the Community.
>
> Any action by the Community shall not go beyond what is necessary to achieve the objectives of this Treaty.

A new article 189b has increased the power of the European Parliament by creating a procedure known as codecision. Under this new procedure Parliament can reject certain kinds of proposed legislation, unless the difference between Parliament and the Council over the proposal can be resolved in a conciliation committee. Other amendments to the EC Treaty were explained when we considered its contents, at pages 4 to 8 above, and it is not necessary to repeat them here.

Title III of the Union Treaty amends the ECSC Treaty in line with the amendments to the EC Treaty. Title IV amends the Euratom Treaty. Title V contains provisions on a Common Foreign Policy and Security Policy; this is the second pillar of Maastricht. Title VI contains provisions on justice and home affairs; this is the third pillar of Maastricht. Title VII contains various final provisions, including article Q which states that the Union Treaty is concluded for an unlimited period.

Annexed to the Union Treaty is a series of declarations and protocols. Two of these have particular importance for the United Kingdom. Protocol 11, on Certain Provisions Relating to the United Kingdom, recognizes that the United Kingdom is not obliged to move to the final stage of monetary union without a separate decision by its government and parliament. Protocol 14, on Social Policy, was necessary because the United Kingdom refused to agree any changes that would have enlarged the power of the

Council to create legislation concerning social policy. The protocol enables the other eleven Member States to use the machinery of the Community to make social legislation amongst themselves: see Chapter 14 of this book.

The Brussels Convention

A survey of the treaties governing the European Community would be incomplete without mention of the Brussels Convention. Article 220 of the EC Treaty states that Member States are to enter into negotiations with each other to obtain agreement on the simplification of formalities governing the reciprocal enforcement and recognition of judgments. It was in pursuance of this article that the Convention on Jurisdiction and Enforcement of Judgments in Civil and Commercial Matters of 27 September 1968 was drawn up. An Accession Convention of 9 October 1978 took account of the enlargement of the Community when Britain joined in 1973. In 1982 a convention was signed to provide for the accession of Greece. A further convention made in 1989 provided for the accession of Spain and Portugal. It now extends to all the Member States of the Community.

Questions relating to the interpretation of the Brussels Convention are referred to the European Court in the same way as questions arising under the EC Treaty. The Convention was incorporated into British law by the Civil Jurisdiction and Judgments Act 1982, which entered into force on 1 January 1987. The text of the Convention is appended to the Act.

The existence of the Brussels Convention means that it is no longer possible to ignore European law. It provides a complete code as to how and when it is possible to sue and enforce judgments in the courts of Member States. A knowledge of the methods of interpretation used by the European Court is essential in order to understand it, and a knowledge of the procedure used by that Court is necessary if any question of interpretation arises.

A consideration of the terms of the Convention is beyond the scope of this book, but the basic rule, subject to a number of specific exceptions, is that persons domiciled in a Contracting State may be sued in the courts of that state, whatever their nationality. The old rule that enabled the British courts to assume jurisdiction simply by reason of the service of a writ within the jurisdiction has now gone.

The Convention is limited to civil and commercial matters. It does not extend to revenue, customs or administrative matters, and does not apply, *inter alia*, to matrimonial property, bankruptcy proceedings and social security. It does extend, however, to matters relating to maintenance; a maintenance creditor can sue in the courts where he or she is domiciled.

The opportunity was taken to amend the Convention on the accession of Spain and Portugal. A consolidated version of the text is to be found in the *Official Journal of the European Communities* (OJ C189 28.7.90 p1).

The Lugano Convention of 16 September 1988 was made between the European Community and the European Free Trade Association (EFTA). It is closely modelled on the Brussels Convention, and allows for the enforcement and recognition of judgments between EFTA states and the Community, but it does not provide any system of appeals to the European Court. It was introduced into English law by the Civil Jurisdiction and Judgments Act 1991.

The Rome Convention

The Convention on the Law Applicable to Contractual Obligations, commonly known as the Rome Convention, was introduced into English law by the Contracts (Applicable Law) Act 1990 and came into effect on 1 April 1990. It provides a complete code as to the law which is to apply to contractual obligations in any situation where there is a choice between the laws of different countries. It differs from the Brussels Convention in that there was no specific provision of the EC Treaty under which it could be enacted, but the preamble speaks of a desire to continue in the field of private international law the work of unification of law which has already been done within the Community. Appeals will lie to the European Court of Justice on questions of interpretation, but at the time of writing the Member States had not ratified the protocols necessary to give this jurisdiction to the Court.

The Convention does not apply to questions of status or legal capacity, wills and succession, rights arising out of matrimonial or family relationships, bills of exchange, arbitration agreements, trusts or certain insurance contracts.

The application of the Convention is not limited to cases where the law of a Member State is applicable, so that a Japanese, for example, will find that the same rules on choice of law apply no matter what forum he uses within the Community.

The European Economic Area Treaty

The European Economic Area Treaty, which was signed on 2 May 1992, is intended to spread the gospel of the single market to the former EFTA countries; it applies to the European Community and Austria, Finland, Iceland, Liechtenstein, Norway and Sweden. Switzerland had a referendum in December 1992 and opted out. By the beginning of 1994 the treaty should have come into effect for all the other signatories, except Liechtenstein which, because of its close relationship with Switzerland, has had to make special arrangements. Freedom of movement for goods, persons, capital, and services will apply throughout the EEA, which will adopt most of the EC single market legislation. The EC rules on competition and state aids have been transposed almost word for word into the treaty, and the EC rules on public purchasing will be applied. There is no automatic referral of cases to the European Court, but the EFTA states can implement a protocol whereby a court in those states will be able to refer a case to the European Court, if it considers it necessary to ask a question on the interpretation of the EEA Treaty or acts adopted in pursuance thereof.

Chapter 2

The Institutions

The main institutions of the Community are the European Parliament, the Commission, the Council of Ministers, the Court of Justice and the Court of Auditors. The Court of Auditors has the task of examining Community accounts and making sure that they are kept regular and legal, but its activities are of little practical interest to lawyers. An important ancillary institution is the Economic and Social Committee, consisting of representatives from trade unions, employers' associations, and consumer groups, which has to be consulted when certain kinds of legislation are made. In this chapter we shall examine briefly the nature of the European Parliament, the Commission, and the Council. The jurisdiction and procedure of the Court of Justice is dealt with in Chapter 5.

The European Parliament

The European Parliament holds its plenary sessions in Strasbourg. It is not entirely powerless, and can sometimes exercise a veto, but it does not yet deserve to be called a parliament because it neither proposes nor makes laws: the Commission proposes legislation, and the Council makes laws.

A proposal from the Commission is rather like a bill in the British Parliament. The proposal is passed on to Parliament which gives an opinion. It comes back to the Commission which takes a view on the opinion of Parliament and then passes it on to the Council.

That used to be the end of matters as far as Parliament was concerned. But new procedures have been devised that must be used for certain kinds of Commission proposals. The Single European Act introduced the cooperation procedure whereby the European Parliament can amend, reject, or approve a common position adopted by the Council. The procedure is now set out in article 189c of the EC Treaty, as amended by Maastricht. Under the cooperation procedure the last word still lies with the Council, however, which can unanimously ignore Parliament if it wishes.

The Maastricht Treaty (the Union Treaty) introduced a new procedure known as codecision. It is set out in a new article 189b of the EC Treaty. Under the codecision machinery the last word, though a negative one, is with Parliament. If Parliament and the Council are unable to resolve their differences the President of the Council and the President of the European Parliament have to convene a conciliation committee. If this fails to reach a compromise Parliament can, in the last resort, reject the proposed legislation.

Some important decisions cannot be made without the assent of Parliament. The assent procedure applies to international agreements which set up institutions, have major financial implications, or require amendment of acts adopted under codecision; and, to certain legislation concerning the uniform electoral system, citizenship, the role of the Central Bank, and structural funds.

The result of having little democracy at the heart of the Community is that it is run by civil servants. We must look at the powers of the Council and, more importantly, the Commission to see what really matters.

The Council

The Council, which has its headquarters in Brussels, is as near as the Community comes to a legislative body. (Do not confuse it with either the Council of Europe, which is the organization that was responsible for the European Convention on Human Rights, or the European Council which is mentioned below.) It is a Council of Ministers of the various Member States of the Community. Thus, if it were discussing agriculture it would be a meeting of ministers of agriculture; if economics a meeting of economics ministers, and so on.

Most decisions are taken by qualified majority, which means that the votes of the various members are weighted; for example, the United Kingdom scores 10 whilst Belgium scores 5. Because ministers are usually employed elsewhere, the day to day work of the Council is done by Council Working Groups of officials taken from the Member States, who assist the Committee of Permanent Representatives of Member States, known as COREPER (Comité des Représentants Permanents). The latter consists of representatives from Member States with ambassadorial rank.

The Council puts the seal on, but does not propose, Community legislation. The Commission proposes legislation which it submits to the Council. The latter must consult the European Parliament and, should the Treaty so stipulate, the Economic and Social Committee. A failure to observe the procedure for consulting the European Parliament may render a measure invalid and liable to be annulled by the Court of Justice.

The Heads of State or of Government of the Community and the President of the Commission meet regularly as a body which is known as the European Council. The European Council has evolved from the regular summit meetings which have taken place between Heads of Government. Article D of the Maastricht Treaty contains a requirement that the Heads of State should meet at least twice a year, so as to provide the European Union with the necessary political impetus. The European Council is not the same as the Council of Ministers but can be regarded as an extension of the latter.

The Commission

The Commission has its headquarters in Brussels and Luxembourg. It proposes Community policy and legislation which is then passed on to the Council for discussion and implementation. The Commission carries out decisions taken by the Council. It is divided administratively into various Directorates General; DG IV, for example, is responsible for competition policy.

It is confusing to find that both the Commission and the Council have powers to make legislation. Both can make regulations and directives, but that does not mean that the Commission acts other than in an executive fashion. For example, the Community law relating to the Common Agricultural Policy consists of a series of basic Council regulations, each of which establishes a common organization of the market for a particular product. But detailed rules for the implementation of these policies are made by the Commission. In Case 25/70 *Köster* [1970] ECR 1161, [1972] CMLR 255 an attempt was made to say that a Commission regulation was invalid because, it was contended, the power to make the regulation lay with the Council and not the Commission. It was said that the Council should have gone through the procedure set out in article 43 of the Treaty. This required the Council to act only on a proposal from the Commission and after consulting the European Parliament. The European Court held that since the Commission did not go beyond the implementation of the basic regulation the Commission regulation was valid. Thus, implementing legislation could be made either by the Commission or by the Council without going through the full procedure of article 43.

The duties and powers of the Commission are set out in article 155 of the EC Treaty, namely: to ensure that the provisions of the Treaty and measures taken by the institutions are applied; to formulate recommendations or deliver opinions on matters dealt with in the Treaty; to have its own power of decision and participate in the shaping of measures taken by the Council and the European Parliament; and to exercise the powers conferred on it by the Council for the implementation of the rules laid down by the Council.

The members of the Commission are Community civil servants. They act in the general interest of the Community, and are completely independent. Article 157 of the Treaty states that they shall neither seek nor take instructions from any Government or any other body.

In article 192 of the EC Treaty we find that the Commission has, amongst other powers, the capacity to impose fines. These fines can be very large, and there are only two months in which to appeal, with no extensions of time. It can also grant interim measures which take effect rather like an interlocutory injunction. For the uninitiated it is rather surprising to find an institution which is not a court, but can impose fines and, in effect, grant injunctions. Such a surprising idea that one can be forgiven a little diversion to look at an example.

Commission Decision (EEC) 87/500, *Brass Band Instruments Ltd* (OJ L286 9.10.87 p36) [1988] 4 CMLR 67, is a decision of the Commission which we will look at again when we examine the Community rules on competition. What happened was that Boosey & Hawkes, the well-known brass band instrument manufacturer, had managed to gain a dominant position in its market, and was therefore in a position to stifle competition. This Goliath of the euphonium was challenged by a David called Brass Band Instruments Ltd.

This little company was set up by former employees of Boosey & Hawkes plc and it hoped to compete in the market by manufacturing and selling instruments directly to brass bands. Brass Band Instruments Ltd complained to the Commission saying that Boosey & Hawkes plc were trying to nip the enterprise in the bud by, amongst other things, refusing to supply parts to its young competitor and withdrawing credit facilities. Such conduct is prohibited by article 86 of the EC Treaty.

The Commission therefore adopted an interim decision which required Boosey & Hawkes plc to supply the parts. The decision went on to say that if they failed to do so they would become liable to a penalty of 1000 ECUs per day. (An ECU is a European Currency Unit, a unit of account which is valued against a basket of European currencies. At the time of writing £1 = 1.3137 ECU.)

The advantages of using the Commission in this way is that it provides a remedy in circumstances where it is difficult to think of a common law action which would be appropriate. It could be cheaper than an action; a mere complaint to the Commission costs nothing. Another lesson to be learned is that this is not only law for Goliaths but can be used by Davids too. The disadvantage is that it tends to be slow, and the Commission much prefers litigants to use national courts if they can; it will only intervene, nowadays, in this kind of case if a point of principle is at stake.

Chapter 3

Legislation

In order to carry out their tasks the Council, Commission, and Parliament jointly with the Council, make regulations, issue directives, take decisions, make recommendations, and deliver opinions. If one regards the EC Treaty as a kind of constitution, then regulations and directives are best seen as rather like our acts of Parliament. They are to be found in large quantities in the *Official Journal*. This is the Community's official gazette but those who are new to Community law will find it difficult to use. Ways of finding your law are discussed in Chapter 4. Article 189 of the EC Treaty explains the nature of the above measures:

- A *regulation* is of general application. It is binding in its entirety and directly applicable in all Member States.
- A *directive* is binding, as to the result to be achieved, upon each Member State to which it is addressed, but leaves to the national authorities the choice of form and methods.
- A *decision* is binding in its entirety upon those to whom it is addressed.
- *Recommendations* and *opinions* shall have no binding force.

Under article 191 of the Treaty, the regulations, directives, and decisions made jointly by Parliament and the Council under the new codecision procedure must be published in the *Official Journal*. These measures come into force on the date specified in them or, if no date is specified, twenty days after publication.

Regulations of the Council and Commission, as well as directives of those institutions that are addressed to all Member States, must be published in the *Official Journal*. They likewise come into force on the date specified in them or, if no date is specified, twenty days after publication.

Other directives and decisions have to be notified to those to whom they are addressed, and take effect upon notification.

Confusion sometimes arises because the ECSC Treaty uses a different vocabulary. Under article 14 of the ECSC Treaty there is a power to make decisions and recommendations. Decisions are binding in their entirety and can be either general or individual in effect. Recommendations are binding as to the aims to be pursued, but leave the choice of methods to the person to whom they are addressed. Therefore, an EC regulation is much the same as an ECSC general decision; an EC directive is similar to an ECSC recommendation; and an EC decision is similar to an ECSC individual decision.

Since a regulation is directly applicable a litigant can, as a general rule, rely upon it directly in an English Court or tribunal; the exceptions are discussed later in this chapter. Directly applicable Community law can be used as a defence; but do not get carried away. In *Application des Gaz S.A.* v. *Falks Veritas Ltd* [1975] 2 CMLR 177 a mere general plea that the plaintiff was abusing a dominant position contrary to article 86 of the EC Treaty was held to be insufficient; it is necessary to give particulars so that the plaintiff will know what case he has to meet.

As well as using a regulation as a defence a plaintiff might use it as a sword and claim an injunction, as was done in *Garden Cottage Foods Ltd* v. *Milk Marketing Board* [1983] 3 CMLR 43, [1984] 1 AC 130. It may be possible to rely on Community law to claim damages, even against a minister, as was tried in *Bourgoin SA* v. *Ministry of Agriculture Fisheries and Food* [1986] 1 CMLR 267, [1986] QB 716. But, as far as English courts are concerned, the extent to which damages may be a remedy, particularly in the context of administrative law, is not entirely clear, although in Cases C–6/90 and C–9/90 *Frankovich* v. *Republic of Italy* and *Bonifaci* v. *Republic of Italy* [1993] 2 CMLR 66, the European Court has said that the state should make good damages caused by its failure to implement Community law.

If the Community law is not clear, any court or tribunal (including, for example, an industrial tribunal or an immigration tribunal) can refer a question to the European Court. Under article 177 of the Treaty, the latter can give preliminary rulings on the interpretation of the Treaty or the validity and interpretation of acts of institutions of the Community. Where the question is raised before a court or tribunal against whose decisions there is no judicial remedy under our law, that is to say a court from which there is no appeal, that court or tribunal must bring the matter before the European Court. The various ways in which it is possible to use Community legislation in an English court are discussed in Chapter 7.

Most Community law is made in the form of directives. This is because it is designed to be absorbed in an indirect way. Community legislation finds its way into our law by the back door in the form of statutory instruments and sometimes statutes. Section 2(2) of the European Communities Act enables ministers or departments to make regulations for the purpose of implementing any Community obligation. This extends to any such provision as might be made by Act of Parliament: for example, a new section 2A and other amendments were introduced into the Equal Pay Act 1970 by the Secretary of State for Employment by means of the Equal Pay (Amendment) Regulations 1983, SI 1983/1794, in order to give effect to Council Directive (EEC) 75/117 (OJ L45 19.2.75 p19) on equal pay. This facility does not include the power to make any provision imposing or increasing taxation or creating criminal offences beyond certain bounds which are set out in Schedule 2 of the Act. An example of a statute which implements a Community directive is the Consumer Protection Act 1987. Various directives in the area of company law have also made profound changes; these are discussed in Chapter 13.

Direct effect

It used to be thought that directives could never have direct effect. A problem arose, however, when it was found that member states were not implementing directives in the way they should. Case 148/78 *Pubblico Ministero* v. *Ratti* [1979] ECR 1629, [1980] 1 CMLR 96 was a case where Italy had been tardy in making legislation to give effect to some Council directives. The Community legislation was designed to eliminate the obstacles to trade between Member States that were caused by different technical requirements over the labelling of chemicals.

Signor Ratti decided to label some of his solvents in accordance with the Community directives. The old Italian law was still in force and he was prosecuted by the Pubblico Ministero for infringement of the Italian law. The Italian court referred the matter to the European Court which ruled that after the expiration of the period fixed for the implementation of a directive a member state may not apply its internal law to a person who has complied with the requirements of the directive. Even if it is provided with penal sanctions, a national law which has not yet been adapted in compliance with the directive could not be enforced.

Thus, directives can have direct effect, at least as between an individual and the state. But it is not in every such case that a directive will have direct effect. You have to look at the general scheme and wording of the directive to see if it imposes clear, complete and precise obligations on the Member State, does not lay down any conditions other than precisely defined ones, and does not leave the Member State any margin of discretion in the performance of its obligations.

The effect of a directive which has become directly applicable is said to be 'vertical'. In other words, it can be used, by a sort of estoppel, as against the state. It cannot be used 'horizontally' against another private individual.

Just to confuse matters, not all regulations are directly effective. It is a matter of interpretation. Not every regulation will be drafted in such a way as to give rights to individuals. It follows that one must examine any Community legislation to see if it passes the test for direct effect.

If the legislation in question is a directive it is necessary to look first for any national laws which implement the directive. If there is a national law available then it may not be necessary to look further. If there is no national law, or if the national law does not come up to expectation, it becomes necessary to consider whether the date for implementation of the directive has passed. This date will usually be about a year after the directive was published; the date will be clearly set out in the text. If that date has passed the directive may confer individual rights, but it can only be used against the state.

Of course, an eagle eye is being kept on the law reports to see how far horizontal effect may have crept into the area of directives, and those who are excited about such things will want to read Case 152/84 *Marshall* v. *Southampton and South West Hampshire Area Health Authority* (152/84) [1986] ECR 723, [1986] 1 CMLR 688 where Miss Marshall complained that, contrary to the Council Directive (EEC) 76/207 (OJ L39 14.2.76 p40) on equal treatment, she was required to retire at 60 instead of 65. She would have been unsuccessful against a private employer because the directive did not have horizontal effect but she was able to recover damages against her employer because the Health Authority was an 'emanation of the state'. The European Court said that:

'Wherever the provisions of a directive appear, as far as their subject matter is concerned, to be sufficiently precise, those provisions may be relied on by an individual against the State where the State fails to implement the directive in national law by the end of the period prescribed or where it fails to implement the directive correctly.'

In Case C–188/89 *Foster* v. *British Gas plc* [1990] ECR I–3313, [1990] 2 CMLR 833 the European Court was not even discouraged to find that the defendant was a private employer. Unlike her male colleagues Mrs Foster was obliged to retire at 60 and, like Miss Marshall, she relied on Directive 76/207 when she sued British Gas plc. She was met by the argument that the defendant was not a state authority, but the Court of Justice held that, nevertheless, British Gas plc had been made responsible by the state for providing a public service under the control of the state, and had special powers beyond those which result from the normal rules applicable in relations between individuals. It followed that she could rely on the direct effect of Community legislation.

It is interesting to consider whether the limits of horizontal direct effect have been yet reached. Would the European Court agree, for example, with the decision in *Doughty* v. *Rolls Royce plc* (*The Times*, 14 January 1992)? In this case the plaintiff was in the same situation as Mrs Foster, and she argued that her employer provided a service, particularly in the area of defence, under the control of the state, but she was unable to persuade the Court of Appeal that Rolls Royce exercised any special powers of the type enjoyed by British Gas.

Academic lawyers, tired of discussing the idea of horizontal direct effect, are now divining a new principle, that of 'useful effect'. Case C–106/89 *Marleasing SA* v. *La Comercial Internacional de Alimentacion SA* [1992] 1 CMLR 305 arose out of a dispute between Marleasing SA and a number of defendants, including La Comercial. The plaintiffs contended that La Comercial was incorporated for no reason but to put the assets of another defendant out of their reach, and that by the law of Spain, which was sensitive to such stratagems, La Comercial did not exist. La Comercial protested that in the First Company Law Directive, Council Directive (EEC) 68/151 (OJ L65 14.3.68 p8), there was an exhaustive list of the only circumstances, none applying to La Comercial, in which a company, by the law of the Community, might be declared to be a nullity. The problem for La Comercial was that the directive had not been implemented in Spanish law, and, since Marleasing SA was not an emanation of the state, it was not possible to rely upon the doctrine of direct effect. But, the European Court rescued La Comercial, by pronouncing that it was for the Spanish court to interpret its law in the light of the wording and purpose of the directive, in order to preclude a declaration of nullity on a ground other than those listed in article 11 of the directive. Thus, La Comercial was able to make use of the directive, which had a useful effect, though it was not directly effective.

Direct effect of Treaty Provisions

Regulations are directly applicable, but what about the Treaty provisions themselves? Clearly it would be a nonsense if the Treaty provisions which give rise to regulations were not directly effective whilst the regulations were. In a series of decisions the European Court has said that certain articles of the Treaty are of direct effect, but not all. Some articles are obviously not of direct effect because they are not designed to give individuals rights. Articles 1 to 4, for example, set out in broad terms the principles of the Community and one would hardly expect them to confer individual rights. Others have been held to be capable of conferring individual rights.

Case 41/74 *Van Duyn* v. *Home Office* [1974] ECR 1337, [1975] 1 CMLR 1 is one of the leading cases on the principles relating to direct effect. It arose out of article 48 of the Treaty which has to do with freedom of movement for workers in the Community; the article was held to be of direct effect. Before a provision can be of direct effect it must be justiciable; in other words, it must be appropriate to be enforced by a court. It must impose a clear, precise, and unconditional obligation, and should not leave a substantial discretion to the Member State. It can be seen that whether it is a directive, a Treaty provision or a regulation the test is the same. In Case 43/75 *Defrenne* v. *Sabena* [1976] ECR 455, [1976] 2 CMLR 98 Mr Advocate-General Trabucchi described the test as follows:

> 'Under the criterion established by the case law of the European Court a Community provision produces direct effects so as to confer on individuals the right to enforce it in the courts, provided that it is clear and sufficiently precise in its content, does not contain any reservation and is complete in itself in the sense that its application by national courts does not require the adoption of any subsequent measure of implementation either by the States or the Community.'

An important point to note, in the *Defrenne* case, is that Miss Defrenne was suing not the state but a company. Treaty articles are capable of having direct effects, not only between an individual and the state, but also between private individuals. Therefore, if a directive does not provide any directly enforceable rights, the litigant may still be able to pray in aid a Treaty article upon which the directive is based. Sometimes it may be possible to use a directive as aid to the interpretation of the Treaty article, and thus achieve the desired direct effect by a circuitous route. This is a method which has been used in some English cases on employment law. Article 119 of the Treaty is of direct effect, and confers the right for men and women to receive equal pay for equal work. Council Directive 75/117 (OJ L45 19.2.75 p19) implements this principle but, in itself, it is not directly applicable except against the state. In *Pickstone* v. *Freemans plc* [1987] 3 WLR 811, [1987] 3 All ER 756 the Court of Appeal so interpreted article 119 in the light of the directive as, effectively, to give the plaintiff the rights she would have had if the directive had direct effect. The decision was later affirmed in the House of Lords but on other grounds.

The task of discovering whether an article in the Treaty is of direct effect is not too arduous. The major text books contain lists of the articles with the relevant cases and the problem is dealt with fully in the section on direct effect in volume 51 of *Halsbury's Laws of England*. Any case concerning an article of the Treaty will inevitably refer to the question of its direct effect.

To add some unnecessary complexity there is academic argument over the difference between 'direct applicability' as used in article 189 and the 'direct effect' which arises because of the criteria established by the case law of the European Court. The Court itself does not always make a distinction.

Chapter 4

Interpretation and Research

Two practical problems face the tyro Community lawyer: how to find his law, and how to interpret it. Not only must he master a new set of research skills, but also acquire the continental manner of interpretation. In this chapter a description is given, with some practical examples, of how to research Community law. But, simply finding the law is not enough. A common lawyer will have a list of common law and equity principles which he applies, almost instinctively, whenever he reads a statute or a case. He will not need to be reminded that equity treats as done that which ought to be done, that statutes are read literally, or that the ratio of the case is binding. Some of these ideas relate to mere interpretation, some to the common law and its philosophy of the freedom of the individual. Community law substitutes its own notions of how legislation should be interpreted, and what basic principles of law and justice it should apply. It interprets legislation by reference to what it considers the legislator has intended, and as basic principles it applies law which is common to all the Member States; equality, certainty, proportionality, natural justice, and fundamental rights are the words used to express these basic principles.

Research

The first place to look for Community law is in one of the standard practitioners' encyclopaedias. It is worth mentioning this because the apoplexy brought on by the realization that a question of Community law has arisen sometimes prevents a lawyer from looking in the obvious place.

Harvey on Industrial Relations and Employment Law (Butterworths) contains a comprehensive section on Community law, including the full text of the Council directives on equal treatment. The *Encyclopaedia of Consumer Law* (Sweet and Maxwell, W. Green and Son) contains the harmonization directives on consumers, as well as the Consumer Protection Act 1987. *Consumer Credit Legislation* (Butterworths) includes Community materials as well as the Consumer Credit Act 1974. Muir Watt: *Agricultural Holdings* (Sweet and Maxwell, Stevens) contains a useful introduction to the subject of milk quotas. *Butterworths Competition Law* contains the text of the EC regulations and directives on competition. *Butterworths Immigration Law Service* contains all of the directives on free movement. *EC Public Procurement* (Longman) contains EC and other international law materials.

Volumes 51 and 52 of *Halsbury's Laws of England* contain a narrative on Community law and have the advantage of a regular update. *Atkin's Court Forms* contains a volume devoted to procedure in the European Court, together with various precedents. *The Digest* (which has long ceased to be the *English and Empire Digest*) contains a volume on Community law, and thus provides a means to research case law in a way familiar to the English lawyer.

Do not forget that Community law is European. Helpful material is published in other languages than English. The encyclopaedia *Le Droit de la Communauté Economique Européenne* (Editions de l'Université de Bruxelles), for example, contains the text of each article of the Treaty followed by an analysis of the text, commentary, implementing legislation and the case law. This approach, which goes by stages from the text of the Treaty to the jurisprudence of the Court, is to be preferred to the approach adopted by most English textbooks.

A large French encyclopaedia, the *Recueils Pratiques du Droit des Affaires dans les Pays du Marché Commun* (Jupiter) contains the Treaty in the five main Community languages. It contains a general introduction to the law relating to each article, and also the texts of the most important regulations and directives. Cases are arranged by Treaty article. It also contains a summary of the relevant national laws. It is therefore a useful source of information of a kind which it is difficult to find elsewhere.

Those with adequate funds will be able to use *LEXIS*, the computer database operated by Butterworths. This contains a library, *EURCOM*, of Community case law in English. The database published by the European Community is called *CELEX*. It is very useful, though expensive, and may be accessed directly or through *LEXIS*. The *CELEX* database contains both Community legislation and the judgments of the European Court. It is possible to use it to reconstruct Community legislation as it was at a particular date, and to see clearly how case law has developed. It is, however, user-hostile and takes time to master. Further information can be obtained from the Office of Official Publications of the European Communities, 2 rue Mercier, L-2985 Luxembourg. The *CELEX* database is also available on CD–ROM in the *JUSTIS* version available from Context Ltd, Tranley House, Tranley Mews, London NW3 2QW. ECJ Law Limited, 17 Lanercost Road, London SW2 3DP publish a database on 3.5-inch disks, updated monthly, which contains summaries of all cases before the European Court and the Court of First Instance since January 1990.

Looking up directives and regulations

No equivalent to *Halsbury's Statutes* exists as an aid to research into Community legislation. Regulations, directives, and decisions, which are sometimes inaccurately called secondary legislation, are to be found in the *Official Journal of the European Communities* (OJ), sometimes referred to by its French initials (JO or JOCE). This is the Communities' official gazette. It is published daily and contains not only the official texts of Community legislation but also draft legislation, official announcements, written questions to the European Parliament, the formal parts of judgments by the European Court, and a variety of other documents.

The Special Edition

The *Official Journal* began in 1958 and was published in the languages of the original Member States. When the United Kingdom joined the Community in 1972 a Special Edition of the *Official Journal* was prepared. The Special Edition is a translation into English of the Community legislation that was still in force when the United Kingdom joined. For this reason the pagination is rather curious. It contains the page numbers of the original publication in the *Official Journal*, but, since not all of the original material is reproduced, there are occasional breaks in continuity. It also has its own continuous pagination. The latter is not supposed to be used for citations, but in practice the page number of the Special Edition is often given.

The Special Edition covers the years 1952 to 1972. When it was prepared the opportunity was also taken to prepare a compilation organised by subject matter. This Subject Edition is a useful reference tool, but unfortunately it has now become out of date. From time to time, however, the Commission publishes compilations of legislation on particular subjects. These are updated regularly and may be obtained from the Office of Official Publications of the European Communities or from HMSO. They are particularly useful when it is necessary to address a court on the contemporaneous state of the legislation. For example, there is a *Guide to Working in a Europe Without Frontiers* (ISBN 92–825–8067–9) dealing with freedom of establishment; and a companion volume, *Freedom of Movement in the Community* (ISBN 92–825–8660–X), both prepared by Jean-Claude Séché. Another useful publication is a collection of measures on company law, *Harmonisation of Company Law in the European Community*, ISBN 92–825–9578–1.

'L' and 'C' series.

Since 1968 the *Official Journal* has been published in two series. The 'L' series contains legislation. The 'C' series contains information, draft legislation, and various notices. Proceedings in the European Parliament are published in an Annex and certain notices to do with public procurement contracts are contained in a supplement.

Until June 1967 the pagination of the *Official Journal* started afresh each year but since that date each daily issue has started with page 1.

Identifying legislation

From 1958 to 1962 regulations were numbered in a single sequence, from number 1 onwards, continuous throughout those five years. So we find that the well known Regulation 17 is referred to as follows:

Council Reg. 17 of 6 February 1962/EEC

From 1963 to 1967 the numbers of regulations begin afresh each year, for example:

Council Reg. 183/64/EEC

Until 1968 Euratom regulations were numbered in the same way as above but in their own sequence. From 1968 onwards all regulations, both of the EC and Euratom, are numbered in a single sequence, the name of the relevant community preceding the number:

Council Reg. (EEC) 4087/88
Council Reg. (Euratom) 1372/72

Directives and decisions before 1962 were not numbered and are referred to simply by the date:

Council Directive of 11th May 1960 (EEC)

From 1963 to 1967 both the EEC and Euratom numbered their directives and decisions in separate sequences beginning at 1 for each year:

Council Dir. 63/226/EEC
Council Dir. 63/27/Euratom

From 1968 both Communities used the same series beginning at 1 for each year:

Council Dir. 77/312/EEC

Carefully note the order in which Community legislation is cited. In the case of a regulation the number precedes the year. In the case of a directive the year precedes the number.

It wise to note that the Community should always be mentioned when legislation is cited or confusion may result. The ECSC uses its own terminology for legislation. The ECSC takes decisions and makes recommendations or delivers opinions. An opinion is not binding and does not count as legislation. An ECSC general decision is similar to an EC regulation. An ECSC individual decision is similar to an EC decision. An ECSC recommendation is similar to an EC directive.

COM documents

Commission working documents consist of reports on implementation of policy, broad policy documents and proposals for legislation, which go through various drafts as they pass from committee to committee. In the early stages these documents are not published, though they may sometimes circulate in samizdat. They are cited as follows:

COM document	Year	Number
COM	(92)	345 FINAL

The example given was a Proposal for a Council Directive amending Directive 71/305/EEC concerning the coordination of procedures for the award of public works contracts, and was published in the *Official Journal* (OJ C225 1.9.92 p13).

A practical example

Let us suppose that the reader wishes to find an item of legislation relating to the free movement of workers. He will find in the library, at the end of the impressive purple row of volumes of the *Official Journal*, a cumulative index. This index is published every six months. It is in two parts. Volume 1 is called the 'Analytical Register'. Volume 2 is the 'Chronological and Alphabetical Index'. It is an index of legislation which is in force. It does not include repealed legislation.

To his dismay the reader will find that the Alphabetical Index is barely alphabetical and hardly an index. It is based on the EUROVOC thesaurus of Community terminology. It consists of broad topics rather than detailed entries. In this it is, however, no different in spirit from Community law which always proceeds from the general to the particular.

Finding the entry for free movement is quite easy, but a particular entry, for hairdressers or dentists for example, will not be found. The entry in the alphabetical index will enable the reader to turn up the relevant page in the analytical register. In the analytical register the titles of all the legislation for a particular topic are grouped together. An item might be listed as follows:

> 68/360/EEC: Council Directive of 15th October 1968 on the abolition of restrictions on movement and residence within the Community for workers of Member States and their families.

Below this entry will be found the *Official Journal* reference and a series of obscure codes which indicate the extent to which the directive has been amended. The key to these codes is in the introduction to the index.

The number of an item of Community legislation is unique and serves to identify it, but it does not enable one to find it immediately in the *Official Journal*. If the number is all that is available one must discover how to use it to find the *Official Journal* reference. The place to look is in the chronological index, which in turn gives the page in the analytical register. The entry in the chronological index, for the above directive, would be as follows:

3	68	L	0360
Code for secondary legislation	Year	Code for directives	Number of directive

A final check on the state of the legislation has to be done rather laboriously by looking through the monthly indexes which are published with the *Official Journal*. The monthly indexes accumulate into a yearly index and are in two parts: an alphabetical index and a methodological table. The methodological table contains lists of the various kinds of legislation which have been published.

The *Official Journal* reference gives the part number, date, and page at which the directive begins:

OJ	L257	19.10.68	p13
Official Journal	Part number	Date of publication	Page on which directive begins

Because the above reference relates to a pre-1972 directive it will be found in the Special Edition in the volume for 1968, part (II). The reference to the Special Edition is written as follows:

Sp edn	1968	(II)	p485
Special edition	Year	Part	Page number for Special Edition

There is no cumulative index to the 'C' series. In order to find proposed legislation and other similar documents it is necessary to look through the annual indexes.

Interpretation

At last the directive has been found. Now the problem is how to interpret it. The common lawyer will, at first, find Community legislation infuriatingly vague. This vagueness is the first barrier to making use of Community law in the English courts.

The secret is that the draftsman proceeds from the general to the particular. If one continues to take Council Directive 68/360 as an example, it will be seen that it begins with a long preamble. The first paragraph of the preamble states that one is to have regard to the Treaty establishing the EEC and in particular article 49. A glance at article 49 will show that it has to do, amongst other things, with systematically and progressively abolishing administrative obstacles so as to bring about freedom of movement for workers as defined in article 48. With this firmly in mind it would be very surprising to find anything in the Directive that contradicted article 48 or 49 of the Treaty.

What is more, if there were some gap that needed to be filled a court would clearly be guided by the purpose which was so clearly and conveniently set out in the Treaty. More help is given by the subsequent paragraphs of the preamble. In the event of a conflict between the wording of the regulation itself and the preamble it is the preamble which will prevail.

Teleological and contextual interpretation

The approach to interpretation which is now favoured by the Court, known as teleological or purposive, is to look at the broad purpose or object of the text. This is quite a natural and obvious method to use, given the way in which Community law is written. It means that literal interpretation does not have the same importance as it does in English law. The Court will, of course, begin with the plain meaning of the words, but where that conflicts with the general scheme and context of the legislation it is the latter which will prevail. The 'plain meaning', moreover, is not the same as the 'literal' meaning.

The Court favours a contextual interpretation. In other words, it will not take an individual article of the Treaty out of context but will have regard to the whole scheme of the Treaty. The Court is not often given to pronouncements upon its methods of interpretation, but in Case 6/64 *Costa* v. *ENEL* [1964] ECR 585, [1964] CMLR 425, a case which is important because it helped to establish the principle of the supremacy of Community law, the contextual method is seen in operation. One of the articles of the Treaty which was considered in this case was article 53, which prevents Member States from introducing new restrictions on the right of establishment. The Court said that article had to be 'considered in the context of the Chapter relating to the right of establishment in which it occurs'. Considered in this way, it was clear that it was capable of creating direct effects between the individual and the state.

An irritation for English lawyers is the frequent absence of a definition section. Partly this is a consequence of the influence of continental legal systems, but there are obviously practical difficulties when Community legislation is written in several languages, each one of which has equal weight when it comes to interpretation. In the search for meaning it is often useful to look at the French version: although all the languages of the Community are equal, French is more equal than others. Legislation will certainly have been prepared, in its early stages, in French. If all else fails one has to look for those cases where the Court has given its interpretation.

Travaux pérparatoires

An abiding fear for the English lawyer is that in search of the meaning of Community legislation he may have to go rooting amongst some obscure bundle of *travaux préparatoires*. It is true that in one instance, Case 6/60 *Humblet* v. *Belgium* [1960] ECR 559, the European Court referred to the opinion of governments put forward during parliamentary debates preparatory to the ECSC Treaty, but it is truly rare for the Court to go to such inordinate lengths.

For practical purposes the problem of deciding what to look at is solved by reference to the preamble. In the preamble to Directive 68/360, for example, it states that the Council had regard to the Opinion of the European Parliament and the Opinion of the Economic and Social Committee and the references to these documents are conveniently given at the foot of the title page of the Directive. Sometimes a directive will refer to the Commission White Paper on Completing the Internal Market or some similar document, or to other directives or regulations; the *Official Journal* reference will usually be given.

General principles

Another problem to cope with at an early stage is the question of what background law the Court will apply. The Court will, of course, look first to the Treaties themselves and the Community legislation made under the provisions of the Treaties. It will also refer to its own case law; for example, the concept of direct effect of directives is law which has been created entirely by the jurisprudence of the Court. Where there are gaps to be filled the Court will look to the fundamental principles of Community law as expressed in the Treaty, such as the right to freedom of movement in article 48 of the Treaty, or to equal treatment in article 119. But, the Court goes further than looking mechanically at the Treaty. It will also refer to general principles common to the laws of Member States.

The most frequently mentioned general principles are these: equality, legal certainty, the protection of legitimate expectations, proportionality, natural justice and fundamental human rights. It is in accordance with these principles that the Court interprets the express provisions of Community law and the legality of Community acts.

The terms used are unfamiliar to a common lawyer. 'Equality' is a principle fundamental to Community law. Its most obvious manifestation is in article 119 of the Treaty which states that men and women should receive equal pay for equal work. It is not, however, confined to discrimination cases, but embraces the general tenet that similar situations must not be treated differently by the law and burdens imposed by the law must be borne equally.

A case often quoted as manifesting how the Court approaches the principle of equality is Case 152/81 *Ferrario* v. *EC Commission* [1983] ECR 2357. Staff of the Commission who were working in Italy complained about the allocation of education allowances. They all sent their children to the same local university but some parents received twice the education allowance of others. This was because the allowance was payable only to those who were entitled to an expatriation allowance. The Court held, however, that the scheme could be objectively justified because expatriates would usually send their children back to their home states for their education. It is interesting to speculate on how the common law would have dealt with this problem: the reasonable man is hardly found in Community law but, if he ever goes there, he will be found looking for objective justification.

'Legal certainty' means that the effect of a provision must be clear, and capable of being predicted. For example, the time limit for bringing proceedings to annul a decision of the Commission is only two months. The time limit may not be extended by the Court even if there is agreement between the parties. The object is that the legal situation should be clear. A striking example of the use of the principle of legal certainty is provided by Case 43/75 *Defrenne* v. *SA Belge de Navigation Aérienne Sabena* [1976] ECR 455, [1976] 2 CMLR 98. In this well known case an air hostess was able to show that, under the Treaty articles relating to equal pay, she was entitled to parity with male cabin staff. That meant that she was able to claim back-pay. Fearful for the economic consequences, however, the Court limited its judgment in such a way that, except for the plaintiff, it was not retroactive. She could claim her back-pay, but for others the right to claim damages for discrimination dated only from the day of the judgment. The principle of legal certainty enabled the Court to *fiat justitia* without *ruat caelum*; justice might be done without risk to the firmament.

The protection of 'legitimate expectation' is an aspect of the principle of legal certainty. It does not have the ineffectual meaning that English courts would attach to the term. Where the conduct of an institution has led an individual to have a reasonable expectation that a certain course will be pursued he may rely upon that expectation. It is a kind of estoppel.

In Case 120/86 *Mulder* v. *Minister van Landbouw en Visserij* [1988] ECR 2321, [1989] 2 CMLR 1, a dairy farmer had been persuaded to give up the production of milk for a year because of a Council regulation designed to encourage farmers to suspend production. In the meantime the Council introduced a system of milk quotas. To his dismay, Mr Mulder found that when he wanted to recommence production he could not obtain a milk quota. This was because he had given up production during the reference period upon which the quota was based. The European Court held that, because he had been encouraged to give up production for a limited period, he could legitimately expect not to be subject to restrictions when he resumed production. The Commission regulation which affected him was held to be invalid, in so far as it did not allocate a quota to him.

'Proportionality' involves the idea that the means used to achieve an end should be no more than what is appropriate and necessary to attain that end. Case 118/75 *State* v. *Watson and Belmann* [1976] ECR 1185, [1976] 2 CMLR 552 is a simple specimen of the use of this principle. Italian law at that time required foreigners to register with the police within three days of entering Italy. This, in itself, was not incompatible with the right to free movement conferred by article 48 of the Treaty; but the Italian legislation also imposed penalties of large fines and, in addition, the possibility of deportation. It was held that Italy was not entitled to impose a penalty so disproportionate to the gravity of the crime that it became an obstacle to the free movement of persons.

'Natural justice' does not differ significantly from the common law concept. It involves the right to be heard, to examine evidence, and to be legally represented. Case 17/74 *Transocean Marine Paint Association* v. *EC Commission* [1974] ECR 1063, [1974] 2 CMLR 459 is a case where, although there was no specific legislative provision which could be said to render the decision invalid, the European Court annulled a decision of the Commission in a competition case. Onerous conditions had been imposed on the plaintiffs. In the long correspondence that led up to the decision the Commission had never mentioned that it proposed to impose such conditions. There was a failure of natural justice because the plaintiffs never had an opportunity to express their point of view.

Closely allied to the principle of natural justice is the idea of respect for fundamental human rights. There is no catalogue of what these human rights may be. They include sexual equality, freedom of religion and the right to a fair hearing. In Case 4/73 *Nold KG* v. *Commission* [1974] ECR 491, [1974] 2 CMLR 338 it was accepted that reference could be made to international treaties which the Member States have signed, as well as the constitutional traditions of Member States. This principle has now found expression in article F of the Union Treaty, which states that the Union shall respect fundamental rights, as guaranteed by the European Convention on Human Rights and Fundamental Freedoms signed in Rome on 4 November 1950, and as they result from the constitutional traditions common to the Member States, as general principles of Community law. In Case 36/75 *Rutili* v. *Minister for the Interior* [1975] ECR 1219, [1976] 1 CMLR 140 it was said, of the human rights enshrined in that Convention, that no restrictions in the interests of national security or public safety might be placed on such fundamental rights unless they are necessary for the protection of those interests in a democratic society.

Case law

Community law has no doctrine of *stare decisis*. This does not mean, however, that it is not possible to see the development of clear lines of authority. A principle, such as direct effect or the Rule in Dassonville (see Chapter 9 of this book) becomes, by constant repetition, predictable; but no rule is immutable.

The jurisprudence of the European Court is published in an official report known as the *European Court Reports* (ECR). These reports contain all the judgments of the European Court, and they are published not only in English but also in the other languages of the Community. The page numbers are the same whether the version used is in English or in another Community language; this makes for great ease of reference.

The *European Court Reports* are full reports that include the submissions of the litigants, but there are great delays in publication. A further disadvantage of the official reports is that they contain only the judgments of the European Court; decisions by the Commission are not included, nor are the judgments of the courts of Member States. The *Common Market Law Reports* (CMLR) are not an official set of reports but have the advantage of prompt publication, contain judgments of the courts of Member States, and also contain some Commission decisions and legislative material.

In competition cases the Commission conducts hearings before a so-called hearing officer. The decisions of the Commission in such cases, coming at the end of a convoluted process involving consultation with the companies concerned, are as important, in many ways, as the judgments of a court. The official texts of these decisions appear in the *Official Journal*.

Reading cases

To a common lawyer the report of a case in the European Court is not a little puzzling. The actual judgment is terse, and affords but little to signify its import. The first thing to read is not the judgment but the opinion of the Advocate General. In the European Court Reports his opinion used to be printed at the end of the report; nowadays it is printed in its logical place, at the beginning. It reads rather like a judgment but one must not mistake it for the judgment.

The function of the Advocate General is discussed in the next chapter; suffice to say, at this stage, that the Advocate General is there to make a reasoned and impartial submission to the Court in order to assist it in coming to the right conclusion. His opinion is, therefore, to be read as if it were the submission of a particularly impartial barrister, instructed as an *amicus curiae*. Consequently, by reading his opinion one may come to a fair understanding of the issues in the case.

The Advocate General is not a judge; though he is of equal status with the judges. His opinion may have great authority. If what he says is the only authority on a point it may be treated as one would the *obiter dicta* of a judge in the common law system. If the judges disagree with him there is still the possibility of arguing that they were wrong. If the judges follow his opinion there is scope for explaining and strengthening the judgment by reference to the opinion. The opinion of the Advocate General is often the best place to begin reading a report because it gives the overall background to the case.

The formal judgment of the Court will begin by reciting the facts, the background law, and the submissions. Before the oral hearing one of the judges, who is referred to as the reporting judge or *juge rapporteur*, will have prepared a report for the Court summarizing the main issues. It is from this report, the *rapport d'audience*, that the opening part of the judgment is prepared. In the next part of the judgment the grounds are given, followed by the formal ruling that constitutes the operative part of the judgment. The logic of this exercise is that, by a gradual process, the issues are distilled to a minimum. The final order therefore impinges precisely on the question in issue.

Chapter 5

The Court

The Court of Justice of the European Communities sits in Luxembourg. It has 13 judges who usually sit in chambers of three or five judges, unless a Member State or Community institution which is party to the proceedings requests it to sit in plenary session. Under article 164 of the EC Treaty the Court has the duty to ensure that in the interpretation and application of the Treaty the law is observed.

In September 1989 a new Court of First Instance was created. Its formation was the result of complaints by the Court of Justice that it was being inundated by staff and competition cases. It is surprising to find that the Treaty, in respect of employees of the Community institutions, required the Court of Justice to exercise the jurisdiction of, in effect, an industrial tribunal. These staff cases came to occupy an inordinate amount of the Court's time. Competition cases also presented a problem because of the enormous quantity of documents involved. Initially the Court of First Instance dealt only with staff cases and competition cases, but in August 1993 its jurisdiction was extended, by Council Decision (Euratom ECSC EEC) 93/350 of 8 June 1993 (OJ L144 16.6.93 p21) to all actions by natural and legal persons brought under articles 173, 175, 178, and 181 of the EC Treaty (and to equivalent proceedings under the ECSC and Euratom Treaties). It is hoped that these reforms, which mean that cases brought by private litigants, as opposed to actions by Member States and Institutions of the Community, will begin in the Court of First Instance, will help to reduce delays. Appeals lie to the Court of Justice on points of law only.

An amendment, made to article 168a of the EC Treaty by the Maastricht Treaty, has given authority to the Council to extend the jurisdiction of the Court of First Instance to such classes of cases as it may determine after a request by the Court of Justice.

In this chapter we shall consider the structure of the European Court, the kinds of action which may be brought before it, and the way in which judgments are enforced. In the next chapter we will consider the rules of procedure.

The Advocate General

To an English lawyer a curious feature of the Court is the role played by the Advocate General. Under article 166 of the Treaty the Court of Justice is assisted by six Advocates General whose duty it is to make reasoned submissions on cases brought before the Court. They act with complete impartiality and independence. During hearings the Advocate General actually sits on the bench with the judges, but to the side of the Court. After the parties have addressed the Court he delivers an opinion which he reads out to the Court. It is prepared, rather like a reserved judgment, after an adjournment. The parties cannot comment on what he says.

His opinion will be found in the law reports, printed alongside the Court's judgment. It is rather similar in style to the judgment of an English judge. As we have seen already, its practical use to lawyers is as a means to divine the likely reasoning of the Court. When reading a judgment of the Court it is best to begin with the opinion of the Advocate General in order to obtain an idea of the facts and issues of law in the case. The opinion of the Advocate General can be used as authority if the Court agrees with him. If the Court does not disagree with him then what he says may still be of persuasive authority. If it disagrees with him his opinion would only be useful in an attempt to show that the Court was wrong.

The *juge rapporteur*

The *juge rapporteur* will be appointed by the President of the Court as soon as the papers arrive. His task is to see the case through the Court. Initially only the *juge rapporteur* will study the papers. He will prepare a preliminary report dealing mainly with procedural issues, such as whether a preliminary inquiry may be necessary. By the time of the hearing he will have prepared a full report which will contain a resumé of the facts and submissions of the parties.

On the day of the hearing the Court will already have read this report. There is, therefore, no need for the advocate for the plaintiff to open the case in the way in which counsel for the plaintiff would begin in an English court; opening the case is a function performed by the *juge rapporteur*.

Types of action

Actions brought before the Court are essentially of two kinds:

direct actions, where Member States, or Community Institutions bring actions against each other; and references under article 177 of the Treaty, that arise when national courts ask the Court of Justice to decide on the interpretation of Community law.

The scope for companies and private individuals to bring direct actions is limited. A private litigant can only bring a direct action against a Community Institution if it has made a decision which is of direct and individual concern to him. In certain circumstances it is possible to sue a Community institution for damages; it is important to understand, however, that it is not possible for one private individual to sue another in the Court of Justice. If a private litigant wishes to raise a point of Community law against another person, he must first bring an action in his national court, and then ask that court to refer the question of Community law to the European Court for its ruling.

The jurisdiction of the Court of Justice is mainly confined to the judicial review of the acts of Community institutions and the interpretation of the Treaty. We shall now examine the various types of action which can be brought before the Court.

Direct actions

Actions against Member States

If the Commission considers that a Member State has failed to fulfil an obligation under the Treaty, then, under article 169 of the Treaty, it has the duty to deliver a reasoned opinion on the matter, after giving the State concerned the opportunity to submit its observations. If the State concerned does not comply with the opinion the Commission may bring the matter before the Court of Justice. The hearing before the Court is not simply a review of the Commission's opinion, but a hearing on all the issues.

An example of the application of article 169 is the well known *German Beer* case, Case 178/84 *EC Commission v. Germany* [1987] ECR 1227, [1988] 1 CMLR 780. In Germany the marketing of foreign beers was prohibited, unless they complied with strict German beer purity laws. The Commission was successful in bringing an action against Germany for the failure to fulfil obligations under article 30 of the Treaty, which prohibits measures having an equivalent effect to restrictions on imports.

If a Member State considers that another Member State has failed to fulfil an obligation under the Treaty, it may bring the issue before the Court under article 170 of the Treaty. Before a Member State brings such an action it has to bring the matter before the Commission. The Commission has to deliver a reasoned opinion, after each of the States concerned has been given an opportunity to submit its own case. If the Commission has not delivered an opinion within three months, the absence of an opinion does not prevent the matter from being brought before the Court.

The judgment of the Court in proceedings under articles 169 and 170 used to be merely declaratory. But now, under article 171 as amended by the Maastricht Treaty, there is a power to impose fines on Member States. The procedure is as follows. If the Commission considers that a Member State has not complied with a judgment of the Court it must, after giving the State an opportunity to submit its observations, issue a reasoned opinion specifying the points on which the Member State has not complied. The Commission may bring the case before the Court of Justice if the Member State fails to take the measures necessary to comply with the judgment. The Court can then impose a lump sum or penalty payment.

Under article 93 there is an infringement procedure in relation to state aids. If, after giving notice to the parties concerned to submit their comments, the Commission finds that aid granted by a State is not compatible with the common market (because it distorts competition or is being misused) it has to decide that the State concerned shall abolish or alter the aid within a period determined by the Commission. If the State does not comply, the Commission or any interested State may refer the matter to the Court; this is in derogation from articles 169 and 170. There is no administrative stage during which the Commission delivers an opinion as there is in articles 169 and 170.

Actions for annulment

The acts of Community institutions are subject to judicial review. Under article 173 of the EC Treaty the Court has the duty to review the legality of the following: acts adopted jointly by the European Parliament and the Council; acts of the Council, of the Commission and of the European Central Bank, other than recommendations and opinions; and, acts of the European Parliament intended to produce legal effects *vis-à-vis* third parties. This jurisdiction is given to the Court in cases brought by Member States, the Council, or the Commission on the following grounds: lack of competence, infringement of an essential procedural requirement, infringement of the Treaty or any rule of law relating to its application, or misuse of power. The Court has jurisdiction under the same conditions in actions brought by the European Parliament and by the Central Bank for the purpose of protecting their prerogatives.

'Lack of competence' means absence of the legal power to adopt an act and is, by its nature, a rare ground. Note that the infringement of a procedural requirement must be of an essential requirement; minor infringements will not be sufficient.

Article 173 includes within in its scope principles analogous to *audi alteram partem* and *ultra vires*. It is wide enough to cover general principles of law which the Court applies, including proportionality (that the end should justify the means), the principle of legal certainty, and equality. The principle of *audi alteram partem* applies even where there is no specific legislative provision: in Case 17/74 *Transocean Marine Paint Association* v. *EC Commission* [1974] ECR 1063, [1974] 2 CMLR 459 part of a decision of the Commission was annulled because, although it contained onerous conditions, no opportunity had been given to the plaintiffs to deal with them in any of the antecedent correspondence.

Any natural or legal person can bring proceedings under article 173, but there are limitations to this jurisdiction. The action can be brought against a decision addressed to the plaintiff. The decision must, however, amount to a legally binding measure. A mere letter from the Commission can be sufficient, provided that it can be shown to bring about a distinct change in the plaintiff's legal position; but, preparatory steps to making a decision cannot be challenged.

Under article 173 an action can also be brought against a decision which, although in the form of a regulation or decision addressed to another person, is of direct and individual concern to the plaintiff. Thus, Community institutions cannot, merely by choosing the form of a regulation, prevent an application by an individual to annul a decision of direct and individual concern to him; the choice of form does not alter the nature of a measure.

A decision will be of direct concern if it does not involve the discretion of some other person. Case 66/69 *Alcan Aluminium Raeran SA* v. *EC Commission* [1970] ECR 385, [1970] CMLR 337 concerned tariff quotas for aluminium. The Belgian government had asked the Commission to open a tariff quota for 1968 under certain provisions derived from the ECSC Treaty. The Commission refused. The question that came before the Court was whether that decision directly concerned three metal importers. The Commission's powers were not unlimited because the Member States kept a large discretionary power. They had a discretion whether to request the quota, and whether or not to open it when it was granted. So the origin of the legal position of the plaintiffs lay not in the decision of the Commission, but in the act of the Member State. It was held that therefore the decision did not directly concern the plaintiff.

The problem of whether a decision was of individual concern was discussed in the *Clementines* case, so called because it concerned an importer of that fruit: Case 25/62 *Plaumann & Co* v. *EEC Commission* [1963] ECR 95 at 107,[1964] CMLR 29. It was said that, in order for a measure to be of individual concern to persons other than those to whom it is addressed, it must affect their legal position because of a factual situation which differentiates them individually in the same way as a person to whom it is addressed.

The time limit for bringing proceedings is short: they must be instituted within two months. The period of two months runs from the date of publication of the measure, or notification to the plaintiff. If there is no publication or notification, it is a period of two months from the day on which the measure came to the knowledge of the plaintiff. There is an extension of time on account of the distance between the Court and the applicant's place of residence which, in the case of the United Kingdom, is 10 days. It is not possible to apply for extensions of time, nor is it possible for litigants to agree an extension of time.

Although the period for bringing actions is extremely short it is unlikely, as a rule, that the litigant will actually have been unaware that a decision was about to be made. In competition cases, for example, a statement of objections is sent by the Commission, and an opportunity is given for the Company concerned to put its case to the Commission before any decision is taken.

If the Court finds that an action under article 173 is well founded, it will declare the act concerned void. In the case of a regulation, however, the Court must, if it considers it necessary, state which of the effects of the regulation which it has declared void shall be considered definitive.

The article 184 exception

The short time limit and the limited *locus standi* under article 173 is mitigated to some extent by article 184 of the Treaty, which enables persons affected by a regulation to challenge it indirectly in proceedings where the regulation is in issue. In French texts this right is referred to as *exception d'illégalité*. There is really no comparable doctrine in English law; it spoils the fruit but does not strike at the root. It might be used in a case where a person was unable to challenge a regulation because he was not directly and individually concerned, but found that he was made the subject of a later decision based upon the regulation. In such a case, he might plead that the regulation was inapplicable on the ground of infringement of an essential procedural requirement, or one of the other grounds set out in article 173. Article 184, as amended, reads:

> Notwithstanding the expiry of the period laid down in the fifth paragraph of Article 173, any party may, in proceedings in which a regulation adopted jointly by the European Parliament and the Council, or a regulation of the Council, of the Commission, or of the ECB is at issue, plead the grounds specified in the second paragraph of Article 173 in order to invoke before the Court of Justice the inapplicability of that regulation.

The sole object of article 184 is to protect an interested party against the application of an illegal regulation, without thereby calling in issue the regulation itself. It cannot, therefore, be used as an action to annul. In the context of the national court it might be raised as an indirect means to challenge Community legislation. The national court would then have to refer the matter to the Court of Justice for a ruling.

In Case 92/78 *Simmenthal* v. *Commission* [1979] ECR 777, [1980] CMLR 25 there is a description of the way in which the remedy works. A number of regulations provided for the common organization of the market in beef and veal, by controlling the price of frozen beef. The plaintiff lacked the *locus standi* to complain about the original regulations because they were not directed to any particular individual. The Commission, acting under these regulations, made a decision fixing the minimum price for frozen beef. The plaintiff was able to challenge the decision on the basis that the enabling legislation was inapplicable.

Actions for failing to act

Article 175 of the Treaty, as amended, provides that should the European Parliament, Council or Commission, in infringement of the Treaty, fail to act, the Member States and other institutions of the Community may bring an action. This kind of action is only admissible if the institution has first been called upon to act. If, within two months, the institution has not defined its position the action can be brought within a further period of two months. The Court regards this remedy as complimentary to article 173. In Case 13/83 *European Parliament* v. *EC Council* [1985] ECR 1513, [1986] 1 CMLR 138 the European Parliament brought an action against the Commission on account of the failure of the latter to legislate for freedom to provide transport services, but there are few examples of similar actions.

Article 175 allows any natural or legal person to complain to the Court where an institution of the Community has failed to act. This might appear to provide a fruitful avenue for private individuals; in fact the jurisdiction in this case is very circumscribed. It only applies where the institution concerned has failed to address an act other than a recommendation or an opinion to the litigant. A regulation is of general effect and would not come within article 175, nor would a directive addressed to a Member State.

Compensation for damage

Under article 215 of the Treaty the contractual liability of the Community is governed by the law applicable to the contract. Article 178 provides, however, that in disputes relating to non-contractual liability the Court of Justice shall have jurisdiction.

Use of this jurisdiction is rare, but an interesting case where the plaintiff was able to recover substantial damages from the Commission is Case 145/83 & 53/84 *Adams* v. *EC Commission* [1985] ECR 3539, [1986] 1 CMLR 506.

In order to understand by what fate Mr Adams was driven to sue the Commission in the European Court it is necessary to refer to an earlier litigation. In 1979 the European Court had given its judgment in Case 85/76 *Hoffman-La Roche* v. *Commission* [1979] ECR 461, [1979] 3 CMLR 211. The Commission had alleged that Hoffman-La Roche had abused a dominant position in the market, contrary to article 86 of the Treaty. The Court recognized that the Swiss multinational's conduct in the market in vitamins could adversely affect both competition and intra-Community trade. The judgment contributed not a little to the liberation of the European market in vitamins.

Mr Adams had been the informant. He had enabled the Commission to uncover the anti-competitive practices of Hoffman-La Roche. The Commission was bound to keep his identity secret. But, owing to the negligence of the Commission's officials, Mr Adam's identity was not kept secret for very long. He was arrested at the Swiss border and, on the basis of a complaint by Roche, charged with the criminal offences under Swiss law of disclosure of business information and breach of business confidentiality. He was granted bail but was ultimately sentenced to a year's imprisonment. The sentenced was suspended. In the European Court he claimed damages for negligence in relation to the breach of confidence by the Commission staff and an award was made in his favour.

Another example of the use of article 178 is Case C104/89 and C37/90 *Mulder* v. *EC Council and EC Commission* [1992] ECR I–3061. This case is explained in Chapter 16 of this book.

Staff cases

Article 179 of the Treaty states that the Court shall have jurisdiction in disputes between the Community and its servants under the conditions laid down in the Staff Regulations or Conditions of Employment. The Court of First Instance deals with these disputes.

Appeals against penalties

By virtue of article 172 of the Treaty the Court has unlimited jurisdiction in relation to penalties provided for in regulations made by the Council or jointly by the Council and Parliament. 'Unlimited jurisdiction' in this context means that the Court has the power not only to annul a penalty but to substitute another. The same unlimited jurisdiction is given to the Court in staff cases and actions for damages. The court is able to go further than merely quashing the matter appealed against. The term does not have the same meaning as the English concept of the unlimited powers or inherent jurisdiction of the High Court.

Arbitrations

The Court of Justice has power, under article 181 of the Treaty, to give judgment pursuant to any arbitration clause in a contract concluded by the Community. It also has jurisdiction in disputes between Member States relating to the Treaty which are submitted to the Court under a special agreement. This area of jurisdiction is little used.

Interim measures

Interim measures are prescribed by the Court under article 186. Such orders are effectively interim injunctions. Article 185 states that actions brought before the Court do not have any suspensory effect. The Court may, however, if it considers that circumstances so require, order the application of the contested act to be suspended.

Referrals

Article 177 of the Treaty states that the Court of Justice is to have jurisdiction to give preliminary rulings concerning the following: the interpretation of the Treaty; the validity and interpretation of acts of the institutions of the Community and of the European Central Bank; and, the interpretation of the statutes of bodies established by an act of the Council, where those statutes so provide. Where such a question is raised before any court or tribunal of a Member State, that court or tribunal may, if it considers that a decision on the question is necessary to enable it to give judgment, request the Court of Justice to give a ruling. Where, however, any such question is raised in a case pending before a court or tribunal of a Member State against whose decisions there is no judicial remedy under national law, that court or tribunal must bring the matter before the Court of Justice.

A referral will usually be the easiest method for the private litigant to bring a case before the Court of Justice. In Case 30/77 *R* v. *Bouchereau* [1977] ECR 1999, [1977] 2 CMLR 800 it was the Magistrates Court which made the reference. Case 41/74 *Yvonne Van Duyn* v. *Home Office* [1974] ECR 1337, [1975] 1 CMLR 1 is well known because it was the first case in which the United Kingdom courts referred a case. Miss Van Duyn asked for a declaration in the Chancery Division that she was entitled under Community law to enter the United Kingdom, and so obtained a reference to the Court of Justice.

A point to note is that when a Court has given judgment it is too late to ask for a reference. Difficulties may arise in the Court of Appeal in this regard because of the need to ask for leave, either of the Court of Appeal or the House of Lords, in order to appeal to the latter court. It is only a court or tribunal against whose decisions there is no appeal that must refer the question to the Court of Justice. It would appear that, where leave is required for an appeal to the House of Lords, it is the Court of Appeal that must make a reference; there is some academic argument over this, but the practical advice is to get your reference as early as possible.

Acte claire

It is not unusual to find resistance on the part of the national court to the idea of a reference. Lord Denning, in *Bulmer* v. *Bollinger* [1974] Ch 401, [1974] 3 WLR 202, tried to lay down guidelines with regard to those cases where it might be appropriate to ask the Court of Justice for a preliminary ruling. He said that unless the point was really difficult or important it would seem better for the English judge to decide it for himself. This view is very unsatisfactory, when seen from a European perspective, because it would lead to the development of different approaches to Community law in different jurisdictions.

The European Court has, in two cases, given some support to the idea that it is not always obligatory for a court to make a reference. In Cases 28-30/62 *Da Costa* [1963] ECR 31, [1963] CMLR 224 it was said to be unnecessary where the point had already been decided in a previous case. In Case 283/81 *CILFIT Srl* v. *Ministry of Health* [1982] ECR 3415, [1983] 1 CMLR 472 the Court went further and said that it was not necessary to make a reference where the point was so obvious as to leave no scope for any reasonable doubt. A reading of these cases will show that the Court is none too enthusiastic about this doctrine which has come to be known as *acte claire*.

Enforcement of judgments

A judgment given against a Member State used to be merely declaratory. When Member States refused to obey the Court the quarrel had to be resolved politically. During the so-called Lamb War lorry loads of English lamb were being hijacked by irate French farmers. The French placed a ban on the import of mutton and lamb from the United Kingdom. Proceedings were brought against France under article 169 of the Treaty and, indeed, France was held to have infringed articles 12 and 30 of the Treaty: Case 232/78 *EC Commission* v. *France* [1979] ECR 2729, [1980] 1 CMLR 418. The French, unabashed, simply refused to comply. A second action was commenced by the Commission, based upon the infringement of article 171 of the Treaty.

Article 171 states that, if the Court of Justice finds that a Member State has failed to fulfil an obligation under the Treaty, the State shall be required to take the necessary measures to comply with the judgment of the Court. But, at that time, there was no power to impose any penalty, and it was a Council compromise in the form of a sheep meat regime which finally ended the litigation.

The position now is different. Article 171, as amended by the Maastricht Treaty, states that if the Commission considers that the Member State concerned has not taken the measures necessary to comply with the judgment of the Court it shall, after giving that State the opportunity to submit its observations, issue a reasoned opinion specifying the points on which the Member State concerned has not complied with the judgment of the Court.

If the Member State concerned fails to take the necessary measures to comply with the Court's judgment within the time limit laid down by the Commission, the latter may bring the case before the Court of Justice. In doing so the Commission has to specify the amount of the lump sum or penalty payment to be paid by the Member State which it considers appropriate.

If the Court of Justice finds that the Member State concerned has not complied with its judgment it may impose a lump sum or penalty payment.

Where a judgment is given in an article 177 case, on a reference to the Court, there is no problem of enforcement. The judgment is simply a step in the proceedings in the court of the Member State and will be enforced automatically in those proceedings.

Actions against Community institutions do not raise practical problems of enforcement. Usually the judgment will be one which results in the annulment of a decision or a regulation, and thus takes effect without the need for further proceedings.

Sometimes proceedings brought by an institution against an individual or a company will result in a money obligation. Article 187 of the Treaty states that judgments of the Court of Justice shall be enforceable under the conditions laid down in article 192. Article 192 states that enforcement is governed by the rules of civil procedure in force in the State where the judgment is carried out. The order for enforcement 'shall be appended to the decision, without other formality than verification of the authenticity of the decision, by the national authority which the Government of each Member State shall designate for this purpose'. In the United Kingdom the application to append the order for enforcement to a judgment is made to the Secretary of State. The High Court is then obliged to register the judgment on application. The procedure is governed by the European Communities (Enforcement of Community Judgments) Order 1972, SI 1972 No 1590, and RSC Ord. 71 rr. 15–24.

The application to register a Community judgment for enforcement is made *ex parte* to the Practice Master. The application must be supported by an affidavit exhibiting the Community judgment, and the order for its enforcement. Execution may not issue without the leave of the High Court until 28 days have expired. During that time an application may be made to vary or cancel registration on the grounds that judgment has been wholly or partly satisfied. If the European Court decides to suspend the enforcement of a Community judgment an application can be made *ex parte* to register that order.

In practice the 'Community judgment' most likely to be registered is not an order of the European Court at all but a decision by the Commission imposing a monetary penalty. Such decisions arise in competition cases. They can be registered by the Commission and enforced like a judgment. If, however, the debtor appeals to the European Court against the Commission's decision and is unsuccessful, it is the order of the European Court which will be registered for enforcement.

Chapter 6

Procedure

The procedures by which, according to the circumstances, European law may be invoked differ widely in scope. There are four possible approaches to consider.

First, an application or complaint may need to be made to the Commission. In competition cases there is a special procedure. This was the method used to obtain Commission Decision (EEC) 87/500, *Brass Band Instruments* (OJ L286 9.10.87 p36) [1988] 4 CMLR 67. This decision has already been described (in Chapter 2) in order to explain the power and nature of the Commission. Brass Band Instruments was a small company which complained about the anti-competitive conduct of a larger company, Boosey and Hawkes. The latter had obtained a dominant position in the market for brass band instruments. Brass Band Instruments applied to the Commission, alleging an infringement of article 86 of the EC Treaty. The complaint was that Boosey and Hawkes had refused to supply them with parts. The Commission was prevailed upon to adopt a decision, as an interim measure, ordering Boosey and Hawkes to supply the parts under pain of a penalty of 1000 ECUs per day.

A complaint to the Commission might be the appropriate avenue where a Member State has adopted a policy which infringes Community law; the protesters who objected to the proposal to build a motorway through Oxleas Wood in Kent used this method, complaining that the Minister of Transport had failed to carry out an environmental assessment in accordance with Council Directive (EEC) 85/337 (OJ L175 5.7.85 p40). For the story of Oxleas Wood see Chapter 15 of this book.

The advantage of a complaint is that it costs nothing. The disadvantage is that it is slow, the Commission has limited resources, and it prefers complainants to pursue remedies in their national courts. In competition cases the Commission has been driven to issue a Notice on Co-operation between National Courts and the Commission in Applying Articles 85 and 86 (OJ C39 13.2.93 p.6). In this notice the Commission points out the advantages of using national courts, namely that the Commission cannot award damages, that national courts can adopt interim measures more rapidly, that national courts can combine EC and national law claims, and that the Commission cannot award costs. The Commission, for its part, intends in future to devote itself to proceedings which have particular political, economic or legal significance. For a more detailed description of this notice the reader should refer to Chapter 12 of this book.

The second approach is by way of a direct action against a Community institution. Usually this will involve an action for annulment brought under article 173; any natural or legal person can bring such an action against a decision of direct and individual concern to him. But, if a Community institution is accused of failing to act the proceedings must be brought under article 175; the Court then has power to order the institution to take the necessary measures.

An irregular decision by the Commission is always susceptible to challenge by a person directly and individually concerned. On the other hand, regulations and directives, because they do not usually directly concern any particular individual, are not easily challenged under article 173; considerable ingenuity is needed to find the *locus standi* for a direct action.

There are two matters well worth remembering in connection with articles 173 and 175: a decision does not have to be a formal document; and, the words 'failure to act' in article 175 have a very restricted meaning. Both matters were considered in Cases 166 & 220/86 *Irish Cement Limited* v. *EC Commission* [1988] ECR 6473, [1989] 2 CMLR 57. The plaintiff had received some aid from the Irish government towards the capital cost of increasing production at its cement works in Limerick. A rival company was awarded a more generous grant to build a cement plant. The plaintiff, therefore, asked the Commmission to institute proceedings against the Irish authorities on the grounds that the money paid to its rival was unlawful state aid and would distort competition. In a letter to the plaintiffs the Commission refused so to do. The plaintiffs contended that the Commission had failed to act.

The Court did not agree. It said that the letter constituted a sufficient action to obviate proceedings under article 175. This was because article 175 refers to a failure to act in the sense of a failure to take a decision or define a position; it does not refer to the adoption of a measure which happens to differ from the one desired by the plaintiff. The Court, nevertheless, remarked that the letter was a decision against which an action to annul might have been brought under article 173. This was not a crumb of comfort to the plaintiff who, alas, had not acted within the two months time limit allowed for bringing annulment proceedings. Thus, the case shows the merits of acting quickly when a direct action is involved, and the narrow scope of an action brought under article 175.

The third possible approach is that an action may be brought in the national court, claiming a breach of some directly applicable provision of Community law. If a question of Community law is in doubt the court will refer it to the European Court under article 177 of the Treaty. This was the method used by Miss Marshall in Case 152/84 *Marshall* v. *Southampton and South West Hampshire Area Health Authority* [1986] 1 CMLR 688, [1986] ECR 723 when she complained that she had suffered unlawful discrimination, contrary to a directive which was designed to afford men and women the right to equal treatment in employment.

A problem that arises when an advocate asks an English court to refer a question to the European Court is that an English judge is prone to regard the whole idea as cumbersome and unnecessary. It is only when a question is raised before a court against whose decisions there is no judicial remedy under national law that a court is obliged to bring the matter before the European Court. A judge at first instance is therefore likely to be reluctant to refer a matter, particularly if he considers the answer to the question is obvious. Indeed, the whole ethos of an English court is to decide the matter then and there. The advocate must be prepared to counter these tendencies; some suggestions as to how this may be done are set out in Chapter 7.

The final way in which Community law is likely to be used is when an action brought in a national court depends upon national legislation which has been created in order to implement a directive. At first sight such an action might appear to be purely domestic in scope; but it will often be found that national legislation does not accurately reflect the requirements of the relevant directive. If the directive is directly applicable it may be possible to rely on it and ignore the national law; but, where the plaintiff is not suing the state, he will be driven to the different tactic of persuading the court to adopt a sympathetic approach to the interpretation of national law, in the light of the underlying Community measure. These problems, which arise when Community law is used in an English court, are dealt with in Chapter 7.

We shall now consider the rules of procedure governing complaints to the Commission, direct actions, and referrals. We will then consider costs, legal aid, and rights of audience. The final topic of this chapter will be the procedural requirements of the Court of First Instance.

Complaining to the Commission

Complaints to the Commission are dealt with in a relatively informal way. As an aid to complainants, however, the Commission has issued a standard complaint form which is obtainable from any of the Commission's information offices. It is also published in the *Official Journal* (OJ C26 1.2.89 p6).

The form requires certain information, namely: the name of the complainant; his nationality; his address or registered office; his sphere of activity; the identity of the Member State, body or undertaking which has failed to comply with Community law; the subject matter of the complaint and damage suffered, if any; the steps taken before national or Community authorities, both administrative and by way of proceedings before courts or tribunals; and, finally, the documentary evidence in support of the complaint. Any individual may lodge a complaint with the Commission. The complaint may either be sent direct to Brussels (Commission of the European Communities, 200 rue de la Loi, B-1049 Brussels) or handed in at one of the Commission's information offices.

An acknowledgement of receipt is sent to the complainant, as soon as the complaint is registered. The complainant is informed of the action taken on his complaint. He is also informed of any infringement proceedings that the Commission intends to institute against a Member State, as a result of the complaint, and of any legal action it intends to take against an undertaking. If proceedings have already been instituted he may, where appropriate, be informed about them.

The Commission will respect confidences; as we have seen, in Case 145/83 *Adams* v. *EC Commission* [1985] ECR 3539, [1986] 1 CMLR 506 an action lay against the Commission for the negligence of its servants in revealing their source of information.

Competition cases

In competition cases the procedure is governed by article 19 of Council Regulation 17 (OJ L13 21.2.62 p204, Sp edn 1959–62 p.87) and by Commission Regulation (EEC) 99/63 (OJ L127 20.8.63

p2268, Sp edn 1963-4 p47). Article 3 of Regulation 17 states that those entitled to make application to the Commission are Member States, and natural or legal persons who claim a legitimate interest; but, the Commission can also act of its own initiative, so that those unable to show strictly that they have a legitimate interest can still complain, and hope that the Commission will take up the cudgels on their behalf.

In competition cases a complaint might be, for example, that there is an agreement or cartel which distorts competition in the Community, or that a company has abused a dominant position in the common market. The complaint does not have to take any particular form; a letter will do. As a general rule, however, the complaint will identify the parties, give details of the infringements of the Treaty, show that the complainant has a legitimate interest, contain any evidence and documents relied on, state what steps have been taken to bring the infringement to an end, and declare that the contents are correct.

The company or undertaking against whom a complaint is made will receive a statement of objections from the Commission identifying the issues. At the same time the Commission fixes the time limit in which the company has an opportunity to reply. The time limit may not be less than two weeks, and may be extended. The Commission will usually inform the company of the contents of its file by means of an annex attached to the statement of objections, although certain documents may be withheld on the grounds of confidentiality.

In its reply the company may set out all the matters relevant to its defence and attach any relevant documents in proof of the facts relied on. If it so requests, in its written comments, the company is entitled to have an oral hearing before the Commission. The hearing is informal, before a hearing officer appointed for the purpose, and the public are not admitted. Minutes are kept which are read and approved by each person heard. Persons appearing before the Commission may be assisted by lawyers. Third parties may be heard if they have a sufficient interest. The outcome of this procedure will be a decision by the Commission. Appeals against such decisions lie to the Court of First Instance.

In Chapter 12 we will return to Regulation 17 in order to examine two other kinds of procedure: for negative clearance, and exemption from the effects of article 85 of the Treaty. These procedures are used where parties have entered into agreements and wish to obtain either an exemption from the competition rules, or an assurance that their agreements do not breach the rules.

Direct actions

Before the Court of Justice of the Community the procedure has two phases: one written, one oral. The written stage consists in the exchange of written pleadings (mémoires) between the parties. This stage is concluded by the preparation of a report by the *juge rapporteur*. The oral stage permits direct contact between the judges and the parties. During this stage the advocates will make submissions in open court and answer questions put to them by the Court. The Advocate General then delivers his opinion, in open court, to the judges. The judges deliberate in private. Finally a single judgment is delivered.

If the Court feels that there is insufficient evidence in the file it may, before the oral stage, order a preliminary enquiry (instruction) which may include the examination of witnesses or the preparation of experts' reports.

Rules of procedure

Certain procedural provisions are to be found in the Statute of the Court of Justice and, under article 188 of the Treaty, the Court has adopted its own rules of procedure which are published in the *Official Journal* (OJ L176 4.7.91 p7).

The written procedure

An action is begun by sending a written application, known as a *requête*, to the Registrar at The European Court of Justice, in Luxembourg. Natural or legal persons, that is to say private litigants, will begin their actions in the Court of First Instance (as to which see below) but the rules of procedure there do not differ in any material way. Service is effected by the Court. The *requête* is referred to in the English version of the rules as a pleading, but it is far wider in scope than that word would imply. Unlike an English pleading it is prepared for the benefit of both the Court and the other parties. It does not have to take any particular form but, under article 19 of the Statute, and article 38 of the Rules of Procedure, the *requête* has to contain the following:

- the name and address of the applicant;
- the designation of the party against whom the application is made;

- the subject matter of the proceedings and a summary of the pleas in law on which the application is based;
- the form of order sought by the applicant;
- where appropriate, the nature of any evidence offered in support.

The 'form of order', meaning a summary of what precisely the litigant is asking the court to do, and what orders he proposes it should make, is not an entirely happy translation of the French word *conclusions*. The conclusions are an essential part of the pleadings. Generally they will be found at the end of the pleading, but the European Court is not given to excessive formalism, so they can be placed elsewhere in the pleadings. They must be sufficiently precise. It is important to ask for costs in the conclusions; it is too late to ask for them during the oral procedure.

No new plea in law may be raised at a later stage in the proceedings. The application therefore delimits the grounds of the claim. But there is no objection to raising, at any stage, new arguments in support of the original pleas in law. Guidance as to what the pleadings should contain is given in Case 4/69 *Lütticke* v. *Commission* [1971] ECR 325, in which the Court said that the pleadings must 'give all the details necessary to establish with certainty the subject matter of the dispute and the legal scope of the grounds invoked in support of the submissions'.

One should note that sometimes problems arise when terms are translated from the French. *Conclusions* is sometimes translated as 'submissions' as well as 'form of order'. The French word *plaidoirie* is sometimes translated as 'pleadings' but is confined to oral submissions.

For the purposes of the proceedings, the applicant has to state an address for service at the place where the Court has its seat (in Luxembourg) and the name of a person who is authorized and has expressed willingness to accept service. The application must be accompanied by the decision it is sought to annul. The lawyer acting for a party has to lodge at the Registry a certificate that he is entitled to practise before a court of a Member State; this certificate can be obtained from the Law Society or the Bar Council.

'A legal person governed by private law', in other words a company, has to lodge with the application some proof of its existence at law. The documents lodged with the application must also contain proof that the authority granted to the applicant's lawyer has been properly conferred on him. If the applicant does not manage to comply with these requirements the Registrar prescribes a reasonable period within which he has to comply; if he fails to comply the Court, after hearing the Advocate General, will decide whether to reject the application.

Every pleading must be signed by the party's agent or lawyer; only Member States or Institutions of the Community will have an agent. If an application is not signed by a lawyer the Court will simply declare it inadmissible. All pleadings have to bear a date, but time runs from lodgment in the Registry. The original pleading, accompanied by all the annexes referred to in the pleading, and five copies plus a copy for every other party, have to be lodged with the Court. Copies have to be certified by the party lodging them. The annexes will consist of a file containing the documentary evidence relied on in support of the application. It is important to understand that it will not be possible to adduce further evidence at the oral stage; all the evidence must be included in the file.

The defendant has one month, after service on him of the application, to lodge a defence. This time limit can be extended by the President on a reasoned request. The defence must state:

- the name and address of the defendant;
- the arguments of fact and law relied on;
- the form of order sought by the defendant;
- the nature of any evidence offered by him.

Other requirements with regard to the defence correspond with those for the application. In the defence it is customary to distinguish between defences on the merits and issues which go to the admissibility of the action. Lawyers in private practice will not usually be called upon to draft defences, since all direct actions are brought against institutions of the Community.

Thereafter there is usually a reply and a rejoinder. The time limits for service of these is set by the President. In a reply or rejoinder a party may offer further evidence but must give reasons for not doing so earlier. Article 42 of the Rules provides that no new plea in law may be raised in the course of proceedings, unless it is based on matters of law or of fact which come to light in the course of the written procedure

Drafting the *requête* requires some degree of care. It defines the issues and contains all the Court will know about the plaintiff's case. There is no rule allowing amendments although in Case 92/78 *Simmenthal* v. *Commission* [1979] ECR 777, [1980] 1 CMLR 25 an amendment was allowed, apparently without comment.

Although a distinction is drawn between raising a new plea in law, which is not allowed, and raising new arguments, which is permitted, there is no rule with regard to departure from the original pleading. Therefore one can plead in reply arguments which, in an English action, might only be dealt with by an amendment of the statement of claim. Be warned, however, that nothing can be added at the hearing.

Because an application must include the law, the facts, and the evidence, in an annexed bundle, it will be much longer than an English pleading. There is, however, no merit in drafting very lengthy pleadings. It is best to be short and to the point. A practical point to note is that although the pleading will be translated for the benefit of the Court, the annexes will not be. It is best to note those annexes which it is essential for the Court to have translated.

The preparatory inquiry

It is the Court which prescribes the measures of inquiry which it considers appropriate. If a party believes that certain facts might be proved by witnesses, or by reference to documents which are not annexed, he should ask for a preliminary enquiry in his pleadings. The *juge rapporteur* prepares a preliminary report upon which the Court will base its order. The Court can order the personal appearance of witnesses, request information and the production of documents, take oral testimony, order experts' reports, and inspect the place or thing in question. Note that the examination of witnesses takes place at the preparatory stage, not during the oral proceedings. In fact it is very rare for there to be any examination of witnesses.

The oral procedure

After the preparatory stage is completed the juge rapporteur will prepare a report for the hearing. This is delivered to the parties' lawyers before the hearing, so that there is an opportunity to correct any inaccuracies. It contains a summary of the facts, and the submissions, of the parties. By the time of the hearing the Court will have read this report, so there is no necessity for the plaintiff to open the case at the hearing. Later on, the report finds its way into the formal judgment in the part headed 'Facts and Issues'.

Advocates appear robed. The judges and the Advocate General are addressed as 'My Lord'. The President of the Court may be addressed as 'Mr President' which will happily translate as *Monsieur le Président*.

Unless the case is very complicated it is unlikely that more than twenty minutes will be allowed for advocacy. It is necessary to speak slowly because everything has to be translated into several languages. The best approach is for the advocate to begin by dealing with any points which were raised in his opponent's last pleading, because there will have been no opportunity to deal with them in any other way. The object of the hearing is to enable the advocate to comment on matters which he was unable to treat in the written pleadings or observations. One or two main points in the case can be emphasized, but there will be little time for flights of rhetoric; often it will be quite acceptable to state, simply, that the submissions are clearly set out in the pleadings and that there is nothing more to add. The Court will want to ask questions, and dealing with them is the most important task. The plaintiff speaks first and there is an opportunity to reply.

Before the case is called on it is customary for counsel to be invited to meet the members of the Court in chambers. This is an opportunity to discuss procedural points, and for the Court to indicate the questions which may be asked.

At the end of the oral hearing the Advocate General may sometimes give his opinion but usually the case is adjourned for several weeks to allow time for him to prepare it. Counsel are not expected to attend when his opinion is delivered. A copy is delivered to them; they cannot comment on the opinion. The judgment of the Court is always reserved; counsel need not attend when this is delivered.

Interlocutory applications

The Court has power to prescribe interim measures under article 186 of the Treaty. Article 185 states that an application to the Court has no suspensory effect but the Court of Justice can, if it considers that circumstances so require, order that application of the contested act be suspended. Article 83 of the Rules of Procedure provides for these applications to be made by a separate document which takes the same form as the main application but must state the subject matter of the proceedings, the circumstances giving rise to urgency and the pleas of fact and law establishing a *prima facie* case for the interim measures applied for.

Sometimes a party will wish the Court to make a decision on a preliminary objection, or on some other procedural issue. Article 91 of the Rules provides for such applications to be made by a separate document, setting out the form of the order sought and the grounds of fact and law relied on. Supporting documents must be annexed to it.

An action will be inadmissible if it is procedurally wrong, out of time, or if there is no *locus standi*. If the defendant considers that an action is inadmissible it will file a short defence raising the preliminary objection. The plaintiff may then file an answer. There is a preliminary hearing. If the defendant is successful that is the end of the matter. If not, the defendant will file a defence in the ordinary way.

Referrals

Under article 177 of the EC Treaty any court or tribunal in a Member State may refer a question to the European Court in order to obtain a ruling. Preliminary rulings under article 177 are, by their very nature, dealt with in a slightly different way to direct actions. Referrals go straight to the Court of Justice; they are never dealt with in the Court of First Instance.

The procedure resembles an appeal by way of case stated. A copy of the reference is sent by the Court of Justice to the parties, to the Member States and to the Commission. They may all submit written observations within two months. The Commission will usually appear at the oral stage and Member States may attend if they are concerned about the outcome.

When a point of Community law is raised before the English High Court the procedure is governed by Order 114 of the Rules of the Supreme Court. An order may be made by the High Court, of its own motion, at any stage of the proceedings. Where an application is made before trial it is made by motion. The order has to set out the request for the preliminary ruling in a schedule which must follow a prescribed form, RSC App.A No.109. The proceedings in which the order is made are stayed, unless the High Court otherwise orders.

Whilst the content of the schedule is ultimately a matter for the court, it is common for the court to ask counsel to draft it. The court may amend the draft as it thinks fit. The rules specify the form of the schedule, and provide that it should set out a clear and succinct statement of the case to enable the Court of Justice to consider and understand the issues of Community law raised, and to enable Member States and other interested parties to submit their observations. The statement should contain:

- particulars of the parties;
- the history of the dispute between the parties;
- the history of the proceedings;
- the relevant facts as agreed by the parties or found by the Court or, failing such agreement or finding, the contentions of the parties on such facts;
- the nature of the issues of law and fact between the parties;
- the English law, so far as is relevant; and
- the Treaty provisions or other Acts, Instruments or Rules of Community law concerned.

There are procedural rules for other courts which require the reference to be sent to the Senior Master of the High Court who waits until the period for lodging an appeal has expired, and then forwards the reference to the European Court: Crown Court Rules SI 1982/1109 r.57; Criminal Appeal (References to European Court) Rules 1972 SI 1972/1786; and County Court Rules, Order 19. No specific rules have been made for the Magistrates Courts.

There are particular procedural problems in the case of jury trials. Once the jury has been empanelled it is not practicable to refer a question to the European Court. However, an EC point can be taken on a motion to quash the indictment, and under section 7 of the Criminal Justice Act 1987 the judge has power, in a serious fraud case, to hear a question of law at a preliminary hearing.

Costs and legal aid

In the case of a referral the costs are a matter for the national court. In direct actions the Court gives a decision as to costs in its final judgment, or in the order which closes the proceedings, provided that the successful party has asked for them in his pleadings; the loser usually pays all the costs.

In the case of a referral in a criminal case legal aid will extend to proceedings before the Court of Justice. The authority for this proposition is *R* v. *Marlborough Street Stipendiary Magistrate ex parte Bouchereau* [1977] 1 CMLR 265, 66 Cr App Rep 195. In the case of a civil action, a legally aided party will need to apply to the Legal Aid Authority for an extension of the legal aid certificate, to cover a referral to the Court of Justice. Under Reg. 51 of the Civil Legal Aid (General) Regulations 1989 SI No 1989/339, the Area Director can amend a certificate where 'it has become desirable for the certificate to extend to ... proceedings in the Court of Justice of the European Communities on a reference to that Court for a preliminary ruling;

or representation by an EC lawyer'. In the case of direct actions there is no provision in the Legal Aid Act 1988 for legal aid to be provided.

The European Court has its own power to grant legal aid. This is quite separate from the ordinary national arrangements with regard to legal aid. An application has to be accompanied by 'a document from the competent authority certifying his lack of means'. The Court makes the order without giving reasons, and there is no appeal. After the hearing, in its decision on costs, the Court can order the assisted party to repay some or all of the legal aid back to the Court.

Rights of audience

In the case of referrals the Court takes account of the national rules so that a lawyer entitled to appear before the referring court will also be able to appear before the Court of Justice. In the case of direct actions private parties must be represented 'by a lawyer entitled to practise before a court of a Member State'; this includes solicitors. Member States and institutions of the Community have to be represented by an agent who 'may be assisted by an adviser, or by a lawyer entitled to practise before a court of a Member State'. University teachers who are nationals of Member States whose law accords them a right of audience have the same rights as are accorded to lawyers entitled to practise before a court of a Member State. These provisions are to be found in article 17 of the Statute of the Court of Justice.

The First Instance Court

Until August 1993 the jurisdiction of the Court of First Instance was limited to staff cases, and competition cases. But, by Council Decision (Euratom ECSC EEC) 93/350 (OJ L144 16.6.93 p.21) its jurisdiction has been extended to actions brought by natural or legal persons under articles 173, 175, 178, and 181 of the EC Treaty, and under corresponding articles of the Euratom and ECSC Treaties. Under article 168a of the EC Treaty, as amended by Maastricht, the jurisdiction of the Court of First Instance can be extended to such further classes of cases as the Council may determine after a request by the Court of Justice.

Some procedural provisions for the Court are set out in the

decision that established the Court of First Instance, Council Decision (ECSC, EEC, Euratom) 88/591 (OJ L319 25.11.88); but, the version originally published in the Official Journal contained several errors, so one should refer to the corrected version (OJ C215 21.8.89 p1). The decision has inserted a new Title IV into the Statute of the Court of Justice. Article 47 of the amended Statute states that where an application, or other procedural document, addressed to the Court of First Instance is lodged by mistake with the Court of Justice it must be transmitted to the other Court and *vice versa*. Where the Court of First Instance or the Court of Justice finds that it does not have jurisdiction it has to refer the matter to the other Court. The Court of First Instance can stay an action where the same issue is being litigated in both Courts at the same time.

The procedure before the Court of First Instance is governed by Title III of the Statute of the Court of Justice and the Rules of Procedure of the Court of First Instance (OJ L136 30.5.91 p1), and *mutatis mutandis* will usually mirror that of the Court of Justice but, unless the case is unusually difficult or important, there is no Advocate General.

Appeals from the Court of First Instance

Appeals from the Court of First Instance to the Court of Justice must be made within two months of notification of the decision appealed against. Appeals are limited to points of law or grounds of lack of competence, breach of procedure before it which adversely affects the interests of the appellant, and infringement of Community law by the Court of First Instance. No appeal lies regarding only the amount of costs. The rules of the Court of Justice require that appeals should be brought by lodging an application at the registry of the Court of Justice or of the Court of First Instance. The application must contain:

- the name and address of the appellant;
- the names of the other parties to the proceedings before the Court of First Instance;
- the pleas in law and legal arguments relied on;
- the form of order sought by the appellant.

An appeal must seek to set aside, in whole or in part, the decision of the Court of First Instance. The appeal must ask for the same form of order, in whole or in part, as was sought at first instance and may not seek a different form of order. The subject matter of the proceedings at first instance may be changed on appeal. A respondent has two months in which to lodge a response which must contain:

- the name and address of the party lodging it;
- the date on which notice of the appeal was served on him;
- the pleas in law and legal arguments relied on;
- the form of order sought by the respondent

The response must seek to dismiss, in whole or in part, the appeal or to set aside, in whole or in part, the decision of the Court of First Instance. It must ask for the same form of order, in whole or in part, as that sought at first instance, and must not seek a different form of order. The subject matter of the proceedings may not be changed in the response.

Chapter 7

Effective Use of Community Law

In the last two chapters the powers of the European Court were considered, and the various procedures by which matters might be brought before that Court. In this chapter the problems which are encountered when European law arises before an English court are considered. These problems include the practical difficulty of persuading the court to refer the matter to the European Court, the manner in which the English Courts interpret national legislation which implements European directives, and the question of what remedies are available for breach of Community law.

Obtaining a reference

What arguments can be raised for a reference? It is not beyond the bounds of possibility that an English court will think that the law is so abundantly obvious that it needs no reference. Lower courts can avoid the issue by refusing a reference and leaving the parties to appeal if they wish: it is only where a question is raised before a court against whose decision there is no judicial remedy that the court must refer the matter to the Court of Justice. But, even there, the courts will try to rely upon the *acte claire* doctrine.

Acte claire is a principle derived from the French courts. It was considered by the European Court, for the first time, in Cases 28–30/62 *Da Costa* [1963] ECR 31, [1963] CMLR 224. It amounts to this, that when the law is so clear as to admit of no reasonable doubt the courts of a Member State are entitled to judge the matter for themselves. Such a doctrine is attractive to the English Court, where the natural reaction of the judge is to decide the matter before him without further ado.

In such a case it may be useful to point out that, although Community Law may seem obvious, the Court cannot know how this law is interpreted in other Member States. Each version of the Treaty is equally authoritative and each version of the regulations and directives. The law of the Community includes general principles from all the Member States. The principle of proportionality, the rule of reason, legal certainty, and legitimate expectation are concepts unknown to the English Court; it is in no way equipped to apply such principles for itself.

The case most frequently referred to in order to illustrate these principles is Case 283/81 *CILFIT* v. *Ministry of Health* [1982] ECR 3415, [1983] 1 CMLR 472. In that case a dispute arose between some wool importers and the Italian Ministry of Health. The dispute concerned the payment of an inspection levy in respect of wool imports from outside the Community. The firms concerned relied on a regulation which prohibited charges having an equivalent effect to a customs duty on 'animal products'. According to the Ministry the scope of the regulation was quite unequivocal and therefore precluded any need to make a reference to the Court for a preliminary ruling.

In the course of the judgment the European Court drew attention to several features of Community law which made it desirable to refer questions to the European Court, even in those cases where the answer might appear to be obvious. The obligation to refer a matter to the Court is based on cooperation, established with a view to ensuring the proper application and uniform interpretation of Community law in all the Member States. It seeks to prevent a divergence of judicial opinion within the Community on questions of Community law.

It is possible that the correct application of Community law may be so obvious as to leave no scope for any reasonable doubt as to the manner in which questions raised are to be resolved; but, before it comes to such a conclusion, the national court must be convinced that the matter is equally obvious to the courts of the other Member States, and to the Court of Justice of the Community. The possibility must be assessed on the basis of the characteristic features of Community law, and the particular difficulties to which its interpretation gives rise. One of the difficulties is that Community law is drafted in several languages and each language is equally authentic. Another difficulty is that Community law uses its own terminology and legal concepts do not necessarily have the same meaning in Community law as in the law of the various Member States.

In *Bulmer* v. *Bollinger* [1974] Ch 401, [1974] 3 WLR 202 the Court of Appeal endeavoured to lay down guidelines as to those cases which might appropriately be referred to the Court of Justice. The suggestion by Lord Denning that the English court should decide the matter for itself when, in the light of all the circumstances, the delay, expense, and the difficulty of the point involved, it was just to do so may not be right when one considers that such a principle would lead to Community law developing along different lines in different jurisdictions. Lord Denning's views seem somewhat old-fashioned in the current European climate.

If delay is raised as an objection it should be emphasized that there is now a new Court of First Instance that has considerably reduced the delay. If cost is an obstacle it should be pointed out that apart from drawing up the question, which has probably been done already, and any written observations which the parties may care to file, a day trip to Luxembourg is probably all that will be needed.

Sympathetic interpretation

There are many cases where neither a direct action nor a reference is appropriate. The Community law may be contained in a directive which has been brought into effect by means of English legislation. The question that then arises is: what is to happen if the English legislation does not follow the intention of the enabling directive?

The academic writers have not been slow to point out that there is a constitutional problem if Community legislation conflicts with the clear words of an English statute. In practice, however, the courts have circumvented the question by interpreting the English statute in sympathy with the European legislation.

The cases that have arisen on this problem nearly all concern article 119 of the Treaty, and various Council directives which have been made in order to confer, *inter alia*, the right to equal pay for equal work. The conflict between British and Community legislation has arisen because of the more advanced approach of the latter to social provisions. The cases on this subject are discussed, in some detail, in the part of this book that deals with social measures, Chapter 14. The cases are best understood when placed in their proper context; but the principles involved are not confined to employment law, and therefore, at the cost of some repetition, the state of the law is summarized in the context of the present discussion.

Three cases in the European Court establish the background of Community law. The first of these is Case 106/77 *Simmenthal* [1978] ECR 629, [1978] 3 CMLR 263. In this case the European Court stated that a national court which is called on, within the limits of its jurisdiction, to apply provisions of Community law is bound to give full effect to those provisions, if necessary refusing to apply conflicting provisions of national legislation, even if adopted subsequently. The case establishes the principle of priority of Community law. It was followed by Case 14/83 *Von Colson* [1984] ECR 1891, [1986] 2 CMLR 430. In the grounds of the judgment in the latter case the Court stated that in applying the national law, in particular the provisions of a national law specifically introduced in order to implement a directive, national courts are required to interpret their national law in the light of the wording and purpose of the directive. In the formal order of the Court the wording is slightly different. There the Court stated: 'It is for the national court to interpret the legislation adopted for the implementation of a directive in conformity with the requirements of Community law, in so far as it is given discretion to do so under national law'. That left a problem over what was to happen if the national law in question antedated the European measure. But in case C–106/89 *Marleasing SA* v. *La Comercial* [1992] 1 CMLR 305 (the facts are related in Chapter 3 of this book) the Court said that in applying national law, whether the provisions in question were adopted before or after the directive, the national court called upon to interpret it is required to do so, as far as possible, in the light of the wording and purpose of the directive, in order to achieve the result pursued by the directive, and thereby comply with article 189 of the Treaty.

The line of English authorities begins with *McCarthy's Ltd* v. *Smith* [1979] 3 CMLR 44 & 381, [1979] 3 All ER 325. In this case Lord Denning, in a dissenting judgment, said that:

'In construing our statutes we are entitled to look to the Treaty as an aid to construction; but not only as an aid but as an overriding force. If on close examination it should appear that our legislation is deficient or is inconsistent with Community law by some oversight of our draftsmen then it is our bounden duty to give priority to Community law.'

In *Garland* v. *British Rail Engineering Ltd* [1983] 2 AC 751, [1982] 2 CMLR 174 Lord Diplock had to construe the words of the Sex Discrimination Act 1975 in the light of the obligation in article 119 of the Treaty. He said that the words of a statute passed after the Treaty are to be construed, if they are reasonably capable of bearing such a meaning, as intended to carry out the obligation which is imposed by the Treaty, and not to be inconsistent with it.

In *Duke* v. *GEC Reliance Ltd* [1988] AC 618, [1988] 2 WLR 359 the plaintiff tried to rely on the words of Lord Diplock, in the above case, in construing the Equal Pay Act in the light of a directive. The equal treatment directive, Council Directive (EEC) 76/207 (OJ L39 14.2.76 p.40), imposes a duty on Britain to implement the principle of equal treatment for men and women in employment. Mrs Duke tried to sue her employer for damages because she was required to retire at 60 instead of 65; but, in this she was unsuccessful, because the House of Lords held that the directive was not of direct effect, and the Equal Pay Act 1970 was not passed in order to give effect to it.

In *Pickstone* v. *Freeman's Publishing* [1989] AC 66, [1988] 3 WLR 265 the House of Lords had, again, to construe the Equal Pay Act 1970. This time the problem was to construe a section which had been inserted in the Act in order to give effect to the equal pay directive, Council Directive (EEC) 75/117 (OJ L45 19.2.75 p19). The method chosen to avoid any difficulty was to adopt a teleological interpretation of the English statute. Lord Keith said: 'It is sufficient to say that the words must be construed purposively in order to give effect to the manifest broad intention of the maker of the regulations and Parliament'.

The importance of those words cannot be underestimated. For the first time an English statute was interpreted in a European way. If this is the method of interpreting such legislation one wonders why British draftsmen should go through the labour of turning perfectly good Community directives into British style statutes. Would it not be simpler to enact them as they stand?

Any doubt that the Pickstone case marked a new departure in the canons of construction was set to rest by the decision in *Litster* v. *Forth Dry Dock Co Ltd* [1989] 2 WLR 634, [1989] 1 All ER 1134. The House of Lords affirmed their earlier judgment. But, neither in this case nor any of the above cases did the House of Lords actually confront the constitutional issues involved in a direct clash between Community law and a British statute.

Disapplying national legislation

In *R* v. *Secretary of State for Transport ex parte Factortame Ltd* [1990] 2 AC 85, [1989] 3 CMLR 1 the problem of what to do when a statute is said to conflict with Community legislation took a startling turn. The appellants were a number of Spanish owners of British trawlers. The Merchant Shipping Act 1988 introduced very strict rules concerning fishing in United Kingdom waters by Community nationals. These rules had the effect of preventing the appellants from using British waters. They asked for judicial review claiming that the law was discriminatory, and consequently contrary to the Treaty of Rome.

Lord Bridge said that by virtue of s.2(4) of the European Communities Act 1972 the Merchant Shipping Act 1988 was to be read subject to directly enforceable Community rights. It was the same as if there was a section in the 1988 Act which said that it was to take effect without prejudice to the directly enforceable Community rights of nationals of any Member State of the Community. It was quite clear that there was a doubt whether the Merchant Shipping Act was compatible with Community law, and that a question should be referred to the European Court.

A problem then arose as to what was to be done in the meantime. It would take two years for the matter to come before the European Court, by which time the appellants would be ruined. As we shall see later in this chapter, it is not entirely certain that there will always be a remedy in damages against the State for breach of Community law, and the European Court of Justice has no power to order interim measures in a case referred to it under article 177 of the Treaty.

The appellants therefore asked the English court for interim relief in the form of an order, pending final judgment, disapplying the Merchant Shipping Act and restraining the Secretary of State from enforcing it against the appellants. The House of Lords refused such interim relief because, said Lord Bridge, it was not possible to obtain an injunction against the Crown in judicial review proceedings, and there was a presumption that English law accorded with Community law until it was declared otherwise.

The European Court of Justice disagreed. In Case C–213/89 *Regina* v. *Secretary of State for Transport ex parte Factortame* [1990] ECR I–2433, [1990] 3 CMLR 375 it said that it is for national courts to ensure the legal protection which persons derive from the direct effect of the provisions of Community law. If the only obstacle which precluded the English court from granting interim relief was a rule of national law, it had to set aside that rule. The House of Lords was therefore obliged to grant an interim injunction, suspending the operation of an act of Parliament.

Remedies in national courts

An injunction can be obtained in an English court for breach of

European law. An example is the case of *Holleran* v. *David Thwaites plc* [1989] 2 CMLR 917, in which the tenants of some tied public houses refused to sign the new tenancy agreement that the brewers had offered them. They claimed that it was contrary to a directive on beer supply agreements, and they were granted an injunction preventing the brewers from exercising their contractual right to claim possession.

But there still remains a problem as to the circumstances in which damages may be obtained in an English court for breach of directly enforceable Community law. In *Garden Cottage Foods Limited* v. *Milk Marketing Board* [1984] 1 AC 130, [1983] 3 WLR 143 it appears to have been accepted that damages would be available against a statutory authority. The Milk Marketing Board is subject not only to British legislation, but also to various Council directives relating to the common organization of the market in milk and milk products. In 1982 the Milk Marketing Board told the appellants that it would no longer be willing to supply bulk butter to them. Garden Cottage Foods Limited brought an action in which it claimed that there had been a breach of article 86 of the EC Treaty. Article 86 forbids the abuse of a dominant position in the market. They asked for an interim injunction. In this they were unsuccessful, although it was not doubted that in an appropriate case an injunction might be granted. Lord Diplock said that, since article 86 was intended not only to promote the general prosperity of the common market, but also to benefit private individuals, to whom loss or damage is caused, it was capable of giving rise to a civil action for damages. Lord Wilberforce seemed reluctant to support this conclusion, but nowadays the case is the first to be cited in support of the proposition that damages are available, in at least a private law context.

In a public law context, the first case to consider is *Bourgoin SA* v. *Ministry of Agriculture* [1986] QB 716, [1986]1 CMLR 267. Some French turkey breeders sued the Minister of Agriculture for damages for refusing to allow the import of their poultry. The minister's action was a breach of article 30 of the Treaty, that deals with free movement of goods. There is a history to this case which is set out in Chapter 9 of this book. The Court of Appeal held that there could be no action against a minister of the Crown for innocently exercising his legislative powers. Although the plaintiffs appealed the action was ultimately settled, so that the position in English law is still not clear.

Until recently the jurisprudence of the European Court did not provide much assistance on the question of whether damages are available against the state. But, in the joined cases C–6/90 and

C–9/90 *Frankovich* v. *Republic of Italy* and *Bonifaci* v. *Republic of Italy*
[1993] 2 CMLR 66 the Court said that the Italian government was
obliged to make good the damage suffered by individuals as a
result of its failure to implement Council Directive 80/987 (EEC)
(OJ L283 28.10.80 p23).

Directive 80/987 is designed to ensure that employees will have
some protection against the loss of their wages, in the form of a
guaranteed payment, in the event of the insolvency of their
employer. Signor Francovich brought an action for his wages
against his insolvent employers, but they had nothing left with
which to pay him. He therefore asked the Italian Republic to pay
him his guarantee; but the government refused to pay him because
it had not implemented the directive. That being so, he sued the
Italian State claiming either that he was entitled to rely upon the
directive, and on that basis must be paid his guarantee, or, alterna-
tively, that he was entitled to damages for the failure to implement
the directive.

His first claim was unsuccessful; the European Court held that he
could not rely upon the words of the directive because it was not
sufficiently precise and unconditional to be directly effective. But
his alternative claim, for damages for failure to implement the
directive, succeeded. The Court said that in order to obtain
damages against the state, for failure to implement a directive, the
following conditions must apply. First, the Directive must be calculated to confer rights on individuals. Secondly, the subject matter
of those rights must be identified by reference to the provisions of
the directive. Thirdly, the existence of a causal link between the
infringement of the obligation incumbent upon the Member State
and the damage suffered must be shown.

The Court also stated that, although it was for the legal system of
each Member State to lay down the procedures to safeguard the
rights of individuals under Community law, the conditions concerning compensation for damage could not be less favourable
than those applicable to similar claims of an internal nature, and
could not be so arranged as to make it virtually impossible or
excessively difficult to obtain compensation.

It might be thought that *Frankovich* simply overrules the decision
of the Court of Appeal in *Bourgoin*, but one must remember that
Frankovich is concerned not with breach of Community law, but a
failure to implement it. In *Bourgoin* the Court of Appeal accepted
that, if the deliberate tort of misfeasance in public office had been
proven, damages against the minister would have been awarded;
the judges justified their decision by saying that the minister was

merely innocently exercising his powers. It follows that the Court of Appeal did not deny that there was a right to obtain damages: they merely circumscribed it. It remains to be seen whether the English rules will be said to be contrary to Community law on the ground that it is virtually impossible, or excessively difficult, to obtain damages.

Unlawful Community Acts

We have seen what happens when national law conflicts with Community law: the national measures can, if necessary, be suspended. But, what is to happen if the converse applies, and it is the European Community measure that is invalid, because, for example, there has been a procedural irregularity? Can a national court, by an interlocutory order, suspend the operation of a Community measure?

The answer is that it can: the circumstances in which a national court may, by an interim order, suspend the operation of an administrative measure based on a Community regulation, are explained in Cases C–143/88 and C–92/89 *Zuckerfabrik Süderdithmarschen AG* v. *Hauptzollamt Itzehoe* [1993] 3 CMLR 1. What happened in this case was that the German Customs Office made a decision requiring Zuckerfabrik Süderdithmarschen AG, a sugar manufacturer, to pay a large levy on its sugar production, under a Council Regulation that was intended to reduce sugar production. The manufacturer appealed to the Finance Court (Finanzgericht) saying that the regulation was invalid. The question referred to the European Court was, whether national courts have the power to suspend the enforcement of national administrative measures adopted on the basis of a Community regulation. The Court replied that the interim legal protection which Community law ensures for individuals must remain the same, irrespective of whether they contest the compatibility of national legal provisions with Community law or the validity of secondary Community law, in view of the fact that the dispute in both cases is based on Community law itself.

But relief may only be granted on the same conditions as the European Court would apply were it dealing with an interim application. Those requirements are as follows: firstly, the court must entertain serious doubts as to the validity of the Community measure, and should refer the question of validity to the European Court; secondly, there must be urgency and a threat of irreparable damage to the applicant; and, thirdly, the national court must take account of the Community's interests, as to whether, for example, suspension of enforcement is liable to involve a financial risk for the Community.

Chapter 8

Pleadings

The European Court has been at pains to prevent undue formalism in its proceedings. There are, however, certain minimum requirements which have to be met and in this chapter we shall consider how to go about drafting an article 177 reference, observations by the parties in such a reference, and an application or *requête* in a direct action.

Article 177 references

The point to keep in mind is that content is more important than form. In this chapter the first example given is of an order made in the High Court for an article 177 reference. This is primarily a matter for the court, but it is customary to call upon counsel to agree the form of the order. *R* v. *Immigration Appeal Tribunal ex parte Antonissen* [1989] 2 CMLR 957 may be usefully referred to as a practical example of the points to bear in mind when requesting the Court to make a reference; the exchange between counsel and the Court is there reported in full.

In Case 141–143/81 *Holdijk* [1982] ECR 1299, [1983] 2 CMLR 635 the European Court gave guidance as to the content of a reference. The information contained in a reference must be sufficient to enable the European Court to consider and understand the issues of Community Law raised, and to enable governments of Member States and other interested parties to make observations. The Commission will usually make observations, even if nobody else does. This advice has now been incorporated into the Supreme Court Rules: see RSC O.114 and the prescribed form, Appendix A No.109.

A reference must contain: particulars of the parties; the history of the proceedings; the relevant facts as agreed by the parties or found by the Court or, failing such agreement or finding, the contentions of the parties on such facts; the nature of the issues of law and fact between the parties; the English law, so far as relevant; and the Treaty provisions or other Acts, Instruments or Rules of Community Law concerned. References from lower courts and references under the Brussels or Rome Conventions will take the same form.

The example that follows is based, very loosely, on Case 138–139/86 *Direct Cosmetics Limited* v. *Commissioners for Customs and Excise* [1988] ECR 3937, [1988] 3 CMLR 333. The case was chosen because it is a practical example of how EC law impinges on practice in the United Kingdom. The issues, much developed in the case, have to do with the circumstances in which the United Kingdom may derogate from the 6th Directive on value added tax. In order to be entitled to make such a derogation the United Kingdom must notify the Commission who may then make the appropriate decision. Those interested in the problem may like to look at *Fine Art Developments plc* v. *Commissioners for Customs and Excise* [1993] 2 CMLR 947, in which an unsuccessful attempt was made to circumvent the Direct Cosmetics case.

A practical point to note is that the *European Court Reports* are the only official reports for the European Court. In pleadings references should be given to these reports rather than the *Common Market Law Reports*.

When a case is filed at the European Court it is given a reference number. Cases are given numbers in chronological order followed by the year, for example '146/77'. When the Court of First Instance was established in 1988 the court registry began to place a letter before the number: 'C', for *Cour*, indicates that the case was heard by the European Court of Justice (e.g. C–999/90), and 'T', for *Tribunal*, indicates that it was heard by the Court of First Instance (e.g. T–999/90).

DRAFT ARTICLE 177 REFERENCE

IN THE HIGH COURT OF JUSTICE   No. . . . .
QUEEN'S BENCH DIVISION

BETWEEN:

> VERY FRILLY TRADERS LTD   Appellant
>
> and
>
> COMMISSIONERS FOR   Respondents
> CUSTOMS AND EXCISE

It is ordered that the questions set out in the Schedule hereto concerning the interpretation of Sixth Council Directive (EEC) 77/388 of 17 May 1977 on the harmonization of laws of Member States relating to turnover taxes – Common system of value added tax: uniform basis of assessment and on the validity of Council Decision (EEC) 85/369 of 13 June 1985, be referred to the Court of Justice of the European Communities for a preliminary ruling in accordance with Article 177 of the Treaty Establishing the European Community.

And it is ordered that all further proceedings in the above mentioned cause be stayed until the said Court of Justice has given its ruling on the said questions or until further order.

SCHEDULE

1. The appellant company is a dealer in frilly items and the respondents are the Commissioners for Customs and Excise, being the body responsible in the United Kingdom for the collection and administration of value added tax.

2. The appellant specialises in direct sales of very frilly items sold through agents in offices, factories and clubs.

3. The scheme operates in the following way. The products are delivered to agents who sell them at the company's catalogue price; if an agent sells a frilly item within 14 days she may retain 20% of the price, but otherwise she must account to the appellant for the full price ... *etc.*

4. The agents are not liable to value added tax because their turnover is below the relevant limit laid down by UK legislation in accordance with article 24 of Directive (EEC) 77/388.

5. As a result of the above trade scheme the final taxable base for the purposes of value added tax is not the final value of sale to the consumer. Consequently no tax is paid on the difference between the final price and the price previously charged ... *etc.*

6. In the United Kingdom the Sixth Directive is implemented by the Finance Act 1977.

7. On the ... of .... 19.. the United Kingdom notified the Commission that a measure derogating from Article 11.A.1(a) of the Sixth Directive had been made by paragraph 3 schedule 4 of the Finance Act 1977.

8. Paragraph 3 of schedule 4 of the Finance Act 1977 reads as follows: 'The Commissioners may by notice in writing ... direct that the value of any such supply shall be ... taken to be its open market value ... *etc.*'

9. Paragraph 3 of schedule 4 is authorized by Council Decision (EEC) 85/369 of 13 June 1985 which was adopted pursuant to Article 27 of the Sixth Directive.

10. On ... of ... 19.. the Commissioners served a notice in the following form directing that the value of goods supplied by Very Frilly Traders Ltd under the above trade scheme should be taken to be the open market value for sale by retail and ... *etc.*

11. The appellants appealed against that notice to the Value Added Tax Tribunal. On the ... day of ... the Tribunal found in favour of the Commissioners. The appellants appealed to the High Court under section 40 of the Value Added Tax Act 1983.

12. The following are agreed facts:

(a) That the trading scheme described above was lawful and was not entered into with a view to avoiding the payment of value added tax.

(b) ... *etc.*

13. The appellants contend that:

(a) Article 27 of the Directive must be interpreted as not permitting a derogating measure where the taxpayer carries on business in a certain manner without any intention to obtain a tax advantage, and that therefore the Commission decision was invalid.

(b) The notice sent to the Commission in accordance with Article 27 of the Directive on the ... of ... 19.. does not mention tax avoidance and that therefore the Decision made by the Commission on ... is invalid.

14. The respondents contend that:

(a) Upon its proper interpretation Article 27 authorizes an exemption because ... *etc.*

(b) Although the notice sent to the Commission referred only to tax evasion the cases mentioned in the notice concerned only tax avoidance and that accordingly the Commission was entitled to make a decision permitting a derogation ... *etc.*

15. The proceedings having been stayed by order of Mr Justice ... on the ... of ..., the Court of Justice, pursuant to the provisions of Article 177 of the Treaty Establishing the European Community, is requested to give a preliminary ruling on the following questions:

(1) Whether, upon the true construction of Article 27 of the Sixth Council Directive (EEC) 77/388 of 17 May 1977, the Commission may adopt a measure derogating from the rule set out in Article 11.A.1(a) of that directive, where the taxable person carries on a business in a particular manner without any

intention of obtaining a tax advantage but for commercial reasons.

(2) Whether a measure that falls outside the terms of the request for authorization made to the Commission under Article 27 of the Directive is invalid.

DRAFT WRITTEN OBSERVATIONS ON AN ARTICLE 177 REFERENCE FOR A PRELIMINARY RULING

IN THE COURT OF JUSTICE   Case C–999/94
OF THE EUROPEAN COMMUNITIES

In the matter of a reference to the Court under Article 177 of the EC Treaty by the High Court of Justice, Queen's Bench Division, for a preliminary ruling in the matter pending before the Court between:

VERY FRILLY TRADERS LTD

and

COMMISSIONERS FOR CUSTOMS AND EXCISE

OBSERVATIONS OF THE COMMISSIONERS FOR CUSTOMS AND EXCISE

On the facts:

1. The facts set out in the reference require explanation. It should be noted that undertakings which have recourse to the methods of trading mentioned therein are not all of the same size and are not equally significant from the point of the functioning of the system of value added tax ... *etc.*

2. Failure to apply the derogating measures would lead to distortion of competition ... *etc.*

Submissions

3. The Commissioners of Customs and Excise have nothing further to add concerning their contentions on the second question set out in the reference.

4. As to the first question, it was said in Case 138–139/86 *Direct Cosmetics Limited* v. *Commissioners for Customs and Excise* [1988] ECR 3937 that ... *etc.*

IN CONCLUSION the Commissioners for Customs and Excise

submit that the questions referred to the Court should be answered as follows:

(1) Article 27(1) of the Sixth Directive permits the adoption of a measure derogating from the basic rule set out in Article 11,A.1(a) of that directive, even where the taxable person carries on business without any intention of obtaining a commercial advantage and for commercial reasons.

(2) There are no factors affecting the validity of Council Decision 85/369 of 13 June 1985 authorizing a derogating measure requested by the United Kingdom.

(*Signature of Counsel*)
Dated ....

Instructed by Solicitors
(*Address for service*)

Pleadings in direct actions

The most frequent example of a direct application is a competition case. Such actions are heard in the Court of First Instance. The rules of procedure with regard to the form and contents of an application are set out in article 44 of the rules of the Court of First Instance (OJ L136 30.5.91 p1), and do not differ materially from the equivalent rule in the Court of Justice, namely article 38 of the Rules of Procedure of the Court of Justice (OJ L176 4.7.91 p7).

The following draft for an application in a direct action is based very loosely upon Case 155/79 *A M & S Europe Ltd* v. *EC Commission* [1982] ECR 1575, [1982] 2 CMLR 264. Such a case would now commence in the Court of First Instance, because it is brought under article 173 of the Treaty by a natural or legal person: see article 3 of Council Decision (ECSC, EEC, Euratom) 88/591 (OJ L319 25.11.88 p1, corrected version OJ C215 21.8.89 p1) establishing the Court of First Instance, as amended by Council Decision (Euratom ECSC EEC) 93/350 (OJ L144 16.6.93 p21). Although no particular form is specified applications will usually be headed by the names of the applicant and defendant, followed by a short title such as 'Application made under Articles 173 and 174 for a declaration that Council Regulation ... is void'. Purists would then begin the body of the pleadings with the words 'May it please the Court to declare that ...' followed by the proposed order in imitation of the French draftsmen. Submissions are then followed by the 'conclusions' or form of the order required. A defence will take the same form as the application, answering each point in turn and containing the conclusion that the application should be dismissed and that the plaintiff should pay the costs. Lawyers in private practice will not be likely to be called upon to draft a defence since the Commission will usually be the defendant.

Since an application has, in itself, no suspensory effect it may be necessary to make a separate application under article 185 and 186 of the Treaty in order to suspend the application of a decision which has been taken. Under article 104 of the Rules of Procedure of the Court of First Instance such an interim application takes the same form as the main application but must state the subject matter of the proceedings, the circumstances giving rise to urgency, and the pleas of fact and law establishing a *prima facie* case for the interim measures applied for.

DRAFT APPLICATION IN A DIRECT ACTION

IN THE COURT OF FIRST INSTANCE OF THE EUROPEAN COMMUNITIES

Between:

Dreadful plc of .... represented by N. Fees QC and C. U. Later Solicitor of Messrs Payup, London with an address for service in Luxembourg at the Chambers of Messrs Paieplus of
....

Applicant

and

Commission of the European Communities, represented by A. Ferret, legal adviser, acting as agent, with an address for service in Luxembourg at the office of G. Fromage, a member of the Commission's Legal Department, Wagner Centre, Kirchberg.

Defendant

Application under Articles 173 and 174 of the EC Treaty for a declaration that Commission Decision .../... of the .... is void

May it please the Court to:

(a) Declare the Commission Decision .../... of 4th July 19.. void.
(b) Order the Defendant to pay the costs.

Points of fact

1. Dreadful plc is a company incorporated in England which manufactures widgets which are sold under the trade name 'Hobson's Choice'.

2. On the 1st January 19.. the Member of the Commission responsible for competition policy directed investigation to be made of the applicant, pursuant to Article 14 of Regulation 17 of the Council.

3. On the 10th January 19.. three officials of the Commission carried out an investigation at the applicant's premises in Bradford the purpose of which was to investigate '... the competitive conditions concerning the production and distribution of widgets in order to certify that there is no infringement of Article 85 and 86 of the EC Treaty'. During the course of the investigation ... etc.

4. At the conclusion of that investigation the officials left the premises taking with them copies of a certain number of documents and leaving with Mr Gradgrind the managing director a written request for further specified documents. The written request states ... etc.

5. By letter dated the 12th March 19.. Dreadful plc sent to the Commission photocopies of certain documents namely ... but at the same time refused to make available others which its legal advisers considered were covered by legal privilege.

6. By decision of 4th July 19.., taken under Article 14(3) of Regulation 17, the Commission required Dreadful plc to produce those specific documents for which legal privilege had been claimed as set out in a schedule ... etc.

7. The decision of the 4th July 19.. requires the applicant to disclose to the Commission's inspector the entire contents of the documents.

8. The Applicant's solicitors gave the following explanation as to why the documents ought to be privileged supported by the documents in the annexed file and listed in the schedule hereto: ... etc.

9. Document ... in the annexed file proves that ... etc.

Submissions

10. The Applicant submits that the documents referred to in the decision of the Commission consisted of letters between an independent lawyer and his client.

11. In Case 155/79 *A M & S Ltd* v. *EC Commission* [1982] ECR 1575 the Advocate General said that . . . the reasoning was followed in . . . etc.

12. The decision was an abuse of power because . . . etc.

13. The applicant submits that the decision was void on the grounds that it was an abuse of power and also contrary to a fundamental principle of Community law, in that it required the production of documents which had been exchanged after the commencement of proceedings, and which were made between a client and an independent lawyer.

Conclusion

May it please the Court to:

(a) Declare the Commission Decision . . . of 4th July 19 . . void.
(b) Order the Commission to pay the costs.

Dated . . . .   (Signature of legal representative)

Chapter 9

Free Movement of Goods

This chapter is concerned with the first of the four freedoms established by the EC Treaty, free movement of goods. Free movement of persons and freedom of establishment are discussed in the next two chapters. Free movement of capital and payments, the subject of articles 67 to 73h of the Treaty, is not dealt with as a separate topic in this book.

The general policy of the Community on free movement of goods is set out in article 3 of the EC Treaty: the elimination, as between Member States, of customs duties and quantitative restrictions on the import and export of goods, and all other measures having equivalent effect. 'Quantitative restrictions' in this context means quotas. The detailed provisions of the Treaty are set out in articles 9 to 37.

Articles 9 to 11 are general measures which state that the Community is to be based upon a common customs union. In relation to third countries a common customs tariff (CCT) is adopted. Products coming from third countries are considered in free circulation in Member States once they have crossed the tariff wall.

Article 12 of the Treaty states that Member States are to refrain from introducing between themselves any new customs duties on exports or imports. A full customs union was achieved by July 1968 so articles 13 to 17, which deal with the abolition of customs duties, are no longer of any practical interest. It is now the concealed and indirect barriers to trade which most concern the Commission.

Articles 30 and 36 are the provisions of the greatest interest. Article 30 prohibits quantitative restrictions on imports and all measures having an equivalent effect. Article 36, typically of Community law, provides for derogations from the general principles set out in article 30. The exceptions provided for by article 36 are those restrictions which can be justified on the grounds, *inter alia*, of public morality, public policy, and public health. Terms encountered in this area of Community law include equivalent effect, the rule of reason, parallel imports, and pro-portionality; an attempt will be made to explain and illustrate these expressions.

Equivalent effect

There is a distinction between the term 'equivalent effect' as it is used, on the one hand, in relation to customs duties and, on the other hand, in connection with quantitative restrictions; although they are clearly connected. First, we shall look at customs duties.

Gingerbread men are a vital element in the economy of Belgium and Luxembourg. This accounts for the Royal and Grand Ducal decrees of February 1960 that increased the special duty levied on the imports of that anthropomorphic confection. The defendants endeavoured to justify the charge by arguing that it was simply the counterpart of internal charges affecting similar domestic products. The Court, in Cases 2 & 3/62 *EC Commission* v. *Luxembourg and Belgium* [1962] ECR 425, [1963] CMLR 199, held that what was important was that the charge jeopardized the objectives of the Treaty and was the result not of a Community procedure, but a unilateral decision. Any duty imposed unilaterally, that applied to a product imported by a Member State, but not to a similar national product, and which, by altering the price, had the same effect on free movement of goods as a customs duty, was unlawful. In Case 158/82 *EC Commission* v. *Denmark* [1983] ECR 3573, [1984] 2 CMLR 658 the charge appeared in the guise of a charge made for the health inspection of peanuts. A charge having equivalent effect to a cus-toms duty was there defined in the following way:

'The Court has consistently held that any pecuniary charge, whatever its designation or mode of application, which is imposed unilaterally on goods by reason of the fact that they cross a frontier, and which is not a customs duty in the strict sense, constitutes a charge having an effect equivalent to a cus-toms duty within the meaning of articles 9, 12, 13 and 16 of the Treaty even if it is not imposed on behalf of the state.'

The case arose because of a Danish law which required importers to pay laboratory charges for health checks on their peanuts. For domestic products such charges were paid for from domestic taxes.

The Court said that charges for health checks were allowed, if they were part of a general system of internal dues, applied systematically, in accordance with the same criteria, to both national products and imported or exported goods. Denmark was unable to show that this was the case. But, charges could be justified on the alternative ground that they represented payment for a service rendered to the importer; provided that the sum charged was in proportion to the service. The idea that justifications will avail only in proportion to their purposes, which is called 'proportionality', is a general one in Community law.

For quantitative restrictions the definition of the meaning of 'equivalent effect' is commonly known as the *Rule in Dassonville.* Monsieur Dassonville had imported some Scotch whisky from France into Belgium. He was prosecuted because he did not have the certificate of origin which was required by Belgian law. French law did not require him to have a certificate, so it is not surprising that he did not have one. The case was referred to the European Court. In Case 8/74 *Procureur du Roi* v. *Dassonville* [1974] ECR 837, [1974] 2 CMLR 436 the European Court formulated the rule as follows:

> 'All trading rules enacted by member states which are capable of hindering directly or indirectly, actually or potentially, intra-Community trade are to be considered as measures having effect equivalent to quantitative restrictions.'

Article 36 excuses

Since the selfish interests of Member States are met by restrictions of imports, they will try to justify their recalcitrance by reference to article 36. The test set out in article 36 is as follows:

> *Article 36.* The provisions of Articles 30 to 34 shall not preclude prohibitions or restrictions on imports, exports or goods in transit justified on grounds of public morality, public policy or public security; the protection of health and life of humans, animals or plants; the protection of national treasures possessing artistic, historic or archaeological value; or the protection of industrial and commercial property. Such prohibitions or restrictions shall not, however, constitute a means of arbitrary discrimination or a disguised restriction on trade between Member States.

The cases on article 36 involve *inter alia* French turkeys, German beer, Dutch wives, and Welsh Sundays.

French turkeys

Case 40/82 *EC Commission* v. *United Kingdom* [1982] ECR 2793, [1982] 3 CMLR 497 is an object lesson in what can go wrong in putting too much trust in exceptions. As a general rule the European Court will construe exceptions narrowly. The background to the case is that the French government was heavily subsidizing French turkey breeders, to the annoyance of English farmers. In 1981 the Minister of Agriculture decided to impose a ban on French poultry imports. The reason was supposed to be an outbreak of Newcastle disease, a dreadful infection of that festive fowl. It was not long before Christmas. The European Court was later to observe that 'certain established facts suggest that the real aim of the 1981 measures was to block, for commercial and economic reasons, imports of poultry products from other Member States, in particular from France'.

The Commission brought proceedings against the United Kingdom alleging a breach of article 30. The United Kingdom lost. As usually happens in this kind of case, the United Kingdom relied on article 36, contending that the ban was justified by reason of protecting the health of British birds. The Court, however, held that such a prohibition must not constitute a means of arbitrary discrimination or a disguised restriction on trade.

That was not the end of the matter. The producers, having established their rights in the European Court, looked around for a remedy; they decided to sue for damages, relying on the direct effect of article 30. In *Bourgoin SA* v. *Ministry of Agriculture Fisheries and Food* [1986] QB 716, [1986] 1 CMLR 267 the Minister of Agriculture found himself being sued for a very large sum of money indeed. It is interesting to see three judges of the Court of Appeal grappling with the argument that article 30 is of direct effect, and that therefore the English courts have a duty to protect that right to the same extent as a domestic right of a similar nature. Only Oliver LJ grasped the nettle that the logic of this must mean damages. Parker LJ and Nourse LJ said that there was no remedy in damages against a minister innocently exercising his legislative powers. It would have been even more interesting to see what the House of Lords and the European Court would have said about it. The plaintiff obtained leave to appeal, but the action was settled for £3.5 million. Nowadays that figure would be even larger because it is assumed, though some quibble remains whether the assumption would always apply in a public law context, that because of the decision in Cases C–6/90 and C–9/90 *Frankovich* v. *Republic of Italy*

[1993] 2 CMLR 66 (see Chapter 7 for the facts) an action for damages will lie against a Member State for its failure to implement Community law.

German Beer

In Case 178/84 *Re Purity Requirements for Beer: EC Commission* v. *Germany* [1987] ECR 1227, [1988] 1 CMLR 780 a complaint was made that German laws stipulated such stringent requirements for the ingredients of beer that foreign brewers could not compete in the German market. It was not that they were prevented from importing their chemical concoctions; it was simply that if they did then, under German law, they were not allowed to call their products beer.

The defence naturally relied on article 36, pointing out the many dangers to healthy German drinkers. The German laws were said to be necessary in order to protect the German consumer from confusion as to what he was drinking, and it was said that the health of the nation might be at risk if German beer drinkers were to drink beers produced, and widely consumed, in other Member States.

Alas, such noble sentiments were to no avail. It was pointed out that the very additives that were forbidden in German beer were generously allowed in soft drinks. German teetotallers did not benefit from solicitude for their health, so, evidently, health was by no means the reason for the beer purity laws. The moral is that when a Member State prohibits the addition of additives to imported beer, but allows them in soft drinks, the prohibition cannot be said to be justified on the grounds of public health within the terms of article 36.

Dutch wives

National predilections can sometimes be discerned in those cases which are considered by the European Court. In Case 121/85 *Conegate Limited* v. *HM Customs and Excise* [1986] 3 ECR 1007, [1986] 1 CMLR 739 the Court had to consider the question which arose when customs officials seized some Dutch wives, variously described as 'Miss World Specials' and 'Rubber Ladies', which were being imported into Britain. Conegate Limited complained that the ban on importation of those articles was contrary to article

30 of the Treaty. The United Kingdom contended that the restriction was justified on the grounds of public morality.

The Court found that the ban on imports was not justified. Although public morality was a matter for each Member State to lay down for itself, it was observed that only the importation of the articles was forbidden; their manufacture was perfectly permissible in the United Kingdom. It followed that, even though the customs legislation was not adopted with the intention of discriminating against goods from Member States, there was, in fact, arbitrary discrimination within the meaning of article 36. A ban on the imports of particular products cannot be justified on the grounds of public morality, within the meaning of article 36 of the EC Treaty, unless comparable restrictions on the domestic sale and manufacture of such products exist and are applied.

The Rule of Reason

A requirement that a product should have 'Made in England', or some such legend, stamped upon it is a venerable way of discouraging imports. Such practices fall within article 30; though not in all circumstances. In Case 120/78 *Rewe-Zentral AG* v. *Bundesmonopolverwaltung für Branntwein* [1979] ECR 649, [1979] 3 CMLR 494, otherwise known as the *Cassis de Dijon* case, the problem was that French liqueurs could not be imported into Germany because of German requirements as to their alcohol content. The Court of Justice held that the fixing of minimum alcohol content for alcoholic beverages fell within article 30, but observed that it would be possible to protect the consumer by requiring an indication of origin, and of the alcohol content, in the packaging of products; but that requirement would have to be subject to the principle of proportionality.

Cassis de Dijon thus deals with the problems which arise when obstacles to movement within the Community result from disparities between national laws relating to marketing of products. In the absence of common rules, on the marketing of alcohol for example, such anomalies are bound to arise, and will be defended by the Member State concerned on laudable grounds such as protection of the consumer. The rule which the Court has developed to deal with such problems is known as the Rule of Reason.

The Rule of Reason is a principle which the Court has developed. It is a justification for conduct which might fall within article 36, but it does not derive from article 36. It is an example of the European

Court filling in gaps. In the *Cassis de Dijon* case the Court expressed the rule as follows:

> 'Obstacles to movement within the Community resulting from disparities between the national laws relating to the marketing of the products in question must be accepted in so far as those provisions may be recognised as being necessary in order to satisfy mandatory requirements relating in particular to the effectiveness of fiscal supervision, the protection of public health, the fairness of commercial transactions and the defence of the consumer.'

Sunday trading

For those who worship Mammon the Shops Act 1950 has been a constant source of irritation, because it restricts the opening of shops on Sunday. What this has to do with article 30 of the Treaty may become clearer to those who have time to consider the arguments in Case 145/88 *Torfaen BC* v. *B&Q plc* [1989] ECR 3851, [1990] 1 CMLR 337. The Borough Council of Torfaen, where tea with the minister after morning Chapel is regarded as an indulgence, prosecuted the defendant company for opening a do–it–yourself store on Sunday. The defence relied on the Rule in Dassonville, because the ban on Sunday trading was, so they said, capable of hindering, directly or indirectly, actually or potentially, intra–community trade. The ban had restricted sales in their shops and had thereby restricted the value of imports from other Member States.

The prosecution relied on the *Cassis de Dijon* case, arguing that the Sunday trading rules were mandatory requirements to do with working conditions, the health and welfare of workers, and typical Welsh Sundays.

A question was therefore referred to the European Court of Justice as to whether the ban on Sunday trading was a measure equivalent to a quantitative restriction on imports. The Court replied that article 30 must be interpreted as meaning that the prohibition which it lays down does not apply to national rules prohibiting retailers from opening their premises on Sunday, where the restrictive effects on Community trade which may result therefrom do not exceed the effects intrinsic to rules of that kind.

Both sides emerged triumphant and promptly fell out over who had won. Another reference to the European Court was necessary to clarify the real issues. The litigants had suffered from two characteristics of the European Court: that upon an article 177 reference it cannot make any findings of fact, and that it will only answer the precise question put. Since the Court hardly troubles itself over whether its answer is helpful, it is incumbent upon the national court to take care how it phrases its questions. In Case C–169/91 *Stoke on Trent City Council* v. *B&Q plc* [1993] 1 CMLR 426, however, it was pointed out that the national court was left in a quandary, if it was asked to make up its own mind as to whether the restrictive effects on Community trade of the Sunday trading rules were disproportionate. The Advocate General said that it was a joint task for the European and the national court to decide whether a national measure was compatible with EC law. But the Court decided to give a simple answer to the question. It ruled that article 30 is to be interpreted as meaning that the prohibition which it lays down does not apply to national legislation prohibiting retailers from opening their premises on Sundays.

Our Sundays are safe. The question to ask oneself is why anyone would ever have imagined a Welsh Sunday would have any effect upon trade within the EC.

Parallel imports

Article 30 applies to the measures of a Member State, but it also affects private arrangements. The cases where this happens are, usually, those involving parallel imports. The situation can happen where, for example, the owner of a patent tries to compartmentalize the market by selling his goods at a higher price in one country than in another. The enterprising trader who slips across the border in order to import goods which have been marketed elsewhere at a lower price is known as a parallel importer.

The parallel importer benefits from article 30. Case 15/74 *Centrafarm BV* v. *Stirling Drug Inc.* [1974] ECR 1147, [1974] 2 CMLR 480 was a case which arose because Stirling Drug was the holder of patents, relating to drugs for urinary infections, in several Community countries. Centrafarm imported the drugs from England and Germany into the Netherlands. The drugs had been put on the market in England by subsidiaries of Stirling Drug. In the Netherlands they could be sold at half the price charged by the owner of the patent. It was held that a patentee could not prevent the import of drugs into a third country where they had already been marketed with his consent. Article 36 could not be relied on in a case where the patent owner had thus volunteered to put his drugs on the unified market.

It used to be thought that article 30 might apply to the conduct of private individuals, such as a policy of stocking only British goods or a campaign to boycott French apples, but in Case 311/85 *Vereeniging van Vlaamse Reisbureaus* v. *Social Dienst van de Plaatselijke en Gewestelijke Overheidsdiensten* [1987] ECR 3801, [1989] 4 CMLR 213 the Court said that articles 30 and 34 of the Treaty concern only public measures, not the conduct of undertakings.

Future developments

The Commission interprets article 7a of the Treaty as meaning that all controls on borders in the Community should be abolished, but the political will to achieve this does not yet exist. The European Parliament, in July 1993, some seven months after the introduction of the single market, found that travellers still had to show passports at EC borders. It has instructed its President to bring proceedings against the Commission for failure to implement the free movement legislation. But, until there is greater cooperation on security and immigration movement within the Community, there will still be restrictions at borders.

Public procurement directives

The right to free movement of goods cannot be viewed in isolation, but must be seen in the light of the rights to freedom of establishment and freedom to provide services which the Treaty guarantees. The relationship is demonstrated by the Community directives on public procurement.

The public procurement directives are intended to make it practicable for businesses throughout the Community to compete for large contracts that are awarded by governments and public authorities. These contracts account for some 15 per cent of the gross domestic product of the Community. Governments and public authorities, if left to their own devices, buy nationally; suppliers from other Member States cannot compete if technical specifications are national in character, or if they are not made aware of the proposed contracts.

The Commission White Paper on Completing the Internal Market (obtainable from HMSO: ISBN 92–825–5436–8) described the continuing partitioning of individual national markets, because of nationalistic policies on public procurement, as one of the most evident barriers to achievement of a real internal market. The system devised by the Commission to end discriminatory practices with regard to the supply of goods and services in the public sector requires that large contracts awarded by public bodies must be advertised in the Official Journal, and be open to tender throughout the Community. But, until the programme of legislation to implement the Single Market in the Community, the rules had no practical effect. This was because the directives contained no effective remedies, and the water, energy, transport and telecommunications sectors were excluded from the regime.

The situation now is that there are three directives setting out fair procedures which must be followed when awarding public works, supply, and service contracts, and one directive, the so called utilities directive, dealing with supply and works contracts in the water, energy, transport and telecommunications sectors.

At the time of writing there were two directives concerning remedies, one for public works and supply, and one for utilities works and supply. As a result of these directives an aggrieved contractor can obtain injunctions or damages if he has been unfairly treated.

In the near future it is expected that consolidating directives will be made because, as will become apparent from the following summary, the directives often go over the same ground, and there are some gaps, such as services in the utilities sector, which need to be filled by amending directives.

Public supply

Public supply contracts, save those awarded by bodies which provide water, energy, transport, and telecommunications services, are governed by Council Directive (EEC) 77/62 (OJ L13 15.1.77 p1) which has been heavily amended by Council Directive (EEC) 88/295 (OJ L 127 20.5.88 p1). These directives apply to contracts for supplies to state regional or local authorities above 200 000 ECUs (130 000 ECUs in the case of certain contracts subject to GATT rules).

The rules are complex, perhaps needlessly so. There are three kinds of procedure which can be used: 'open', where any interested supplier can present an offer, 'restricted', where only those suppliers invited to do so may submit tenders, and 'negotiated', where contracting authorities consult suppliers of their choice and negotiate terms with one or several of them.

The restricted procedure can only be used in cases justified *inter alia* by the specific nature of the products or the need to maintain a balance between contract costs and procedural costs. Negotiated procedures are only to be used in exceptional cases, such as where there is no response to an open procedure, cases of extreme urgency, or where articles are manufactured for research purposes. Technical specifications have to be defined by reference to national standards implementing European standards, or common standards (drawn up with a view to uniform application in all the Member States). There are time limits during which tenders must remain open. Contracts have to be advertised in the *Official Journal*. Unless justified by the contents of the contract, contractual clauses which mention goods of a specific make are forbidden.

Public works contracts

Contracts for public works awarded by the state, regional or local authorities have been subject to Community rules since 1971, under Council Directive (EEC) 71/305 (OJ L 185 15.8.71 p5, Sp edn 1971 (II) p682). This directive has now been extensively amended by Council Directive (EEC) 89/440 (OJ L210 21.7.89 p1). Broadly, the object of this amendment, which had to be implemented by July 1990, was to bring public works contracts into line with the new directives on public supply. The directive, as amended, applies to contracts above the value of 5 000 000 ECUs.

Fixed procedures have to be adhered to in awarding public works contracts. There are three procedures, 'open', 'negotiated', and 'restricted', as in the case of public supply contracts. Contracts must be advertised in the *Official Journal*. There was a good deal of confusion as to who was governed by the directive, which applies to entities 'governed by public law'. In the United Kingdom there is, of course, no systematic body of public law. The amendments, however, set out a non-exhaustive list which includes education authorities, fire authorities and police authorities.

The directive does not apply to contracts awarded by concerns operating in the water, energy, transport and telecommunications sectors.

Public service contracts

Public service contracts are dealt with by Council Directive (EEC) 92/50 ((OJ L209 24.7.92 p1) which came into effect on 1 July 1993.

This applies to contracts between service providers and contracting authorities, excluding entities operating in the water, energy, transport and telecommunications sectors, of not less that 200 000 ECUs. It also applies to design contests for contracts of not less than this value. On the continent design contests are the more popular way of awarding contracts for town planning, architectural or civil engineering projects.

The procedures to be followed are largely the same as those for works and supply.

The utilities

Public entities which administer water, energy, transport and telecommunications were once excluded from the above purchasing regime. Contracts for both works and supplies in these sectors are now covered by Council Directive (EEC) 90/531 (OJ L297 29.10.90 p1), which imposes similar obligations to those to be found in the other directives, but is not limited to public authorities. The newly privatised water and electricity industries have to take account of it; some aspects, in particular the lack of secrecy and the bureaucracy, are not necessarily to their commercial advantage. The directive does not apply to air transport.

The threshold values for this directive are 400 000 ECUs for supply contracts in energy and transport, 600 000 ECUs for telecommunications supply, and 5 000 000 ECUs for all works contracts. The rules may not be subverted by splitting up contracts.

The utilities directive has introduced the concept of attestation, that is to say a system whereby the purchasing systems of concerns are audited on a regular basis so as to ensure compliance with the law.

Remedies

Article 30 of the Treaty does provide the possibility of some remedy for discriminatory purchasing practices. Thus in Case 45/87 *EC Commission* v. *Ireland* [1988] ECR 4929, [1989] 1 CMLR 225 the Dundalk District Council published a notice in the *Official Journal* inviting tenders for a contract to lay pipes for its water system. The specification for the contract said that the supplier had to be certified as manufacturing pipes to the Irish Standard. In fact there was only one manufacturer so certified. As it turned out there never had been a need to place a notice in the *Official Journal*, because at that time the utilities directive had not been implemented. The European Court found that, nevertheless, there was a breach of article 30 of the Treaty, because the specification had an effect equivalent to a restriction on imports.

The need for a more effective and rapid remedy than that afforded by making a complaint to the Commission is provided by the so called remedies directives. Council Directive (EEC) 89/665 (OJ L395 30.12.89 p33) is implemented in the United Kingdom by the Public Supply Contracts Regulations 1991, SI 1991 No 2679, and the Public Works Contracts Regulations, SI 1991 No 2680. These two statutory instruments set out not only the procedure to be followed in awarding public contracts, but also the remedy for failure to comply with either the regulations themselves or the laws of the Community. Proceedings must be brought in the High Court; the supplier must inform the contracting authority beforehand of the breach and his intention to bring proceedings, and proceedings must be begun within three months of the breach. The High Court can make an interim order suspending the award procedure, set aside a decision, and award damages.

Council Directive (EEC) 92/13 (OJ L76 23.3.92 p14) provides for remedies in the utilities sector. This is implemented in the Utilities Supply and Works Contracts Regulations 1992, SI 1992 No 3279.

As an alternative to litigation the directives and the implementing legislation provide for a conciliation procedure in which the Commission will, if requested, appoint a conciliator. In the United Kingdom the request must be sent to the Treasury for onward transmission to the Commission.

Chapter 10

Free Movement of Persons

The EC Treaty draws a distinction between freedom of movement for workers, which is covered by articles 48 to 51, and the related rights of establishment and freedom to provide services which are to be found in articles 52 to 66.

The Maastricht Treaty has introduced a new concept, namely citizenship of the Union; a new Part Two of the Treaty has been created for this purpose. Article 8 of the Treaty, as amended by Maastricht, states that citizens are to enjoy the right to move freely within the Community, but subject to the limitations and conditions laid down in the Treaty. Citizenship sounds grand, but it is not the same as nationality; the right to move freely within the Community is limited.

Freedom to move from one Member State to another usually depends upon whether the person claiming the right is a worker, is establishing himself in another Member State, or is a provider or recipient of services; those who do not come within these categories must show that they have enough resources not to become a burden on the social security systems of their host states. Restrictions can only be placed on free movement on grounds of public policy, public security, or public health. Problems arise over the meaning and scope of the terms 'worker', 'public policy', and 'services'.

British legislation was slow to take account of the rights conferred by Community law but the Immigration Act 1988 eventually grudgingly recognized that persons exercising enforceable Community rights do not require leave to enter the United Kingdom. Most of the various regulations and directives on freedom of movement for persons in the Community are conveniently gathered together in a publication available from the Office of Official Publications of the European Communities or HMSO: *Freedom of Movement in the Community, Entry and Residence*, by Jean-Claude Séché, ISBN 92–825–8660–X. Butterworths *Immigration Law Service* also contains a complete collection of EC legislation, regularly updated, together with extracts from a selection of cases.

Workers

Article 48 of the Treaty establishes the right to freedom of movement for workers in the Community. This freedom entails the abolition of any discrimination based on nationality, as regards employment, remuneration, and conditions of work. It also entails the right, subject to limitations on grounds of public policy, public security, or public health, to accept offers of employment actually made, to move freely within Member States for this purpose, to stay in a Member State for the purposes of employment, in accordance with the provisions governing the employment of nationals of the state, and to remain there after having been employed. But, article 48 does not apply to employment in the public service.

In Case 66/85 *Lawrie-Blum* v. *Land Baden Württemberg* [1986] ECR 2121, [1987] 3 CMLR 389 a worker was defined as a person who for a period of time performs services for, or under, the direction of another person, and receives remuneration in return. The practical problem faced by criminal law practitioners is that their clients usually do not work in the accepted sense of the term. Case 118/75 *Watson* v. *Belmann* [1976] ECR 1185, [1982] 2 CMLR 552 seems to imply that it is possible to recognize, as workers, those who have not previously received an offer of employment in another state. A similar sentiment was expressed in Case 48/75 *Royer* [1976] ECR 497, [1976] 2 CMLR 619; but the extent to which Community law protects those who look for work but find none is not clear. Under the provisions of the present Immigration Rules, which have been made under the Immigration Act 1971, a national of a Member State loses his right to remain if he does not acquire employment within six months. In Case 292/89 *R* v. *Immigration Appeal Tribunal ex parte Antonissen* [1991] 2 CMLR 373 ECJ the European Court had to consider whether this restriction was contrary to Community law. It ruled that a national of a Member State who has not found work after six months may be required to leave unless he provides evidence that he is continuing to seek employment and has a genuine chance of being engaged.

Council Regulation (EEC) 1612/68 (OJ L257 19.10.68 p2, Sp edn 1968 (II) p475) has been made with the object of giving effect to the free movement provisions in the Treaty. This regulation provides that any national of a Member State has the right to take up an activity as an employed person within the territory of another Member State. Workers who are not nationals of a Member State do not have this right, but the regulation provides that, irrespective of their nationality, members of a worker's family are entitled to install themselves with a worker who is a national of one Member State and who is employed in another.

The family, for these purposes, extends to a spouse and their dependents, under the age of 21, and dependent relatives in the ascending line. The Immigration Act 1971, by contrast, does not give an automatic right of entry to a spouse. The Home Office rules made under the Act prevent a spouse obtaining entry clearance where the primary purpose of the marriage is to obtain entry. It follows that a man who is not a Community national, who marries a woman who is a British citizen, will not be able to join her as of right in the United Kingdom, but he will be able to join her in another Member State, if she exercises her right of free movement to go there. The question was decided in C–370/90 *R* v. *Immigration Appeal Tribunal and another ex parte Secretary of State for the Home Department* [1992] 3 All ER 798, in which the husband Mr Surinder Singh, an Indian national, married a British wife and they went to live in Germany. They returned to the United Kingdom in order to open a business. But the marriage failed and a decree nisi was granted. His limited leave to remain was cut short and he was ordered to be deported. The Court of Justice held, on a reference from the Divisional Court, that article 52 of the Treaty and Council Directive (EEC) 73/148 (OJ L172 28.6.73 p14)) require a Member State to grant leave to enter and reside in its territory to the spouse, of whatever nationality, of a national of that state who has gone, with that spouse, to another Member State in order to work there as an employed person, as envisaged by article 48 of the Treaty, and returns to establish herself or himself as envisaged by article 52 of the Treaty in the state of which he or she is a national. A spouse must enjoy at least the same rights as would be granted to him or her under Community law if his or her spouse entered and resided in another member state. But Cases 35,36/82 *Re Morson and Jhanjan* [1982] ECR 3723, [1983] 2 CMLR 221 show that the Treaty pro-visions on free movement of persons cannot be applied unless there is a factor which links them to the situations which are governed by Community law. So Mr Tombofa, a Nigerian national against whom the Home Secretary made a decision to deport after he was convicted of an attempted robbery, was unable to take advantage of the EC rules when he married a United Kingdom citizen. His counsel's hopeful submission that his wife was a recipient of services because she listened to Radio Luxembourg, so bringing into play the directive which implements the right to free move-ment in relation to establishment and services, Council Directive (EEC) 64/221 (OJ L56 4.4.64 p850, Sp edn 1963–64 p1150), was rejected: *R* v. *Secretary of State for Home Affairs ex parte Tombofa* [1988] 2 CMLR 609 CA.

The right of retired and incapacitated workers, and their families, to remain in the territory of a Member State, after having been employed there, is dealt with in Council Regulation (EEC) 1251/70 (OJ L 142 30.6.70 p24, Sp edn 1970 (II) p402). But, in *R* v. *Secretary of State for the Home Department ex parte Botta (Jacqueline)* [1987] Imm AR 80, [1987] 2 CMLR 189 the Court of Appeal said that where a wife from a country which is not a Member State had come to the United Kingdom with a German national she could not remain here after her husband was deported.

Council Directive (EEC) 68/360 (OJ L 257 19.10.68 p13, Sp edn 1968 (II) p485) makes provisions for documentation. Article 3 of this directive provides that Member States shall allow workers, and their families, to enter their territories simply on production of a valid identity card or passport. No entry visa or equivalent may be demanded, save from members of the family who are not nationals of Member States. Member States are obliged to accord to such persons every facility for obtaining any necessary visas. As proof of the right of residence a document entitled 'Residence Permit for a National of a Member State' has to be issued which must include a statement that it is issued pursuant to Regulation (EEC) No 1612/68. It is proposed to amend this directive so as to make the formalities simpler; instead of a permit there will be a European Communities Residence Card (OJ C100 21.4.89 p8).

Public policy

The meaning of 'public policy' is expanded by Council Directive (EEC) 64/221 (OJ 56 4.4.64 p850, S edn 1963-64 p1150) which applies to the employed, self-employed, and recipients of services. The directive relates to all measures concerning entry, issue or renewal of residence permits, or expulsion taken by Member States on grounds of public security, or public health. Such grounds must not be invoked to serve economic ends. They must be based exclusively on personal conduct. Previous criminal convictions do not in themselves constitute grounds for the taking of such measures. Expiry of an identity card or passport does not justify expulsion.

The concept of public policy was discussed in one of the first United Kingdom cases to be referred to the European Court: Case 41/74 *Van Duyn* v. *Home Office* [1974] ECR 1337, [1975] 1 CMLR 1. At that time it was not obvious that all the above legislation is of direct effect. Miss Van Duyn, a Dutch national, claimed that she was entitled to enter the United Kingdom and remain there in order to take up employment at the Hubbard College of Scientology. She asked for a declaration in the Chancery Division, and a number of questions were then referred to the Court of Justice. The European Court held that the provisions of article 48 of the Treaty and Directive 64/221 were directly effective; but the United Kingdom had acted lawfully because membership of the Church of Scientology constituted 'conduct', within article 3 of the latter directive, of a kind which would justify a refusal of leave to enter.

The concept of public policy in Community law was also examined in Case 36/75 *Rutili* v. *Minister for the Interior* [1975] ECR 1219, [1976] 1 CMLR 140. That was a case where the French Minister for the Interior had imposed on an Italian National restrictions that prohibited him from living in certain French departments. It transpired that the reason for this was his trade union activities, which were regarded as 'likely to disturb public policy'.

On a reference to the Court of Justice it was said that the concept of public policy must be interpreted strictly, so that its scope cannot be determined unilaterally by each Member State without being subject to control by the institutions of the Community. Article 6 of the Treaty prohibits discrimination on the grounds of nationality, and it followed that measures restricting rights of residence may not be imposed, except in cases where such measures are equally applied to the nationals of a Member State.

Case 30/77 *Regina* v. *Bouchereau* [1977] ECR 1999, [1977] 2 CMLR 800 was a reference from the Marlborough Street Magistrates Court. M. Bouchereau was a French national who had been convicted of possession of a small quantity of drugs. He was fined £35 but the magistrate was minded to recommend his deportation. The Court of Justice ruled that the mere fact that a crime had been committed, or that there were previous convictions, was not enough to constitute grounds for deportation; there had also to be 'a genuine and sufficiently serious threat affecting one of the fundamental interests of society'.

In Cases 115 & 116/81 *Adoui and Cornaille* v. *Belgium* [1982] ECR 1665, [1982] 3 CMLR 631 two French waitresses were refused a permit to live in Belgium. It was alleged that the ladies worked in a bar where it was suspected that immoral things went on. The Belgian court, in a reference to the European Court, asked for a definition of public policy.

The Advocate General seemed somewhat piqued at this question. He said that the first point to emphasize was that Community law does not define or purport to give an independent definition of public policy. In the Community Treaties there are numerous expressions derived from the laws of the Member States whose interpretation involves reference to principles, rules, and concepts peculiar to those States. The expression 'public policy' fell within that category. Within national legal systems there were areas of uncertainty. It was therefore pointless to ask the Court for a definition of public policy. The Court ruled, however, that a Member State could not refuse access to its territory by reason of conduct which was not subject to repressive measures in respect of its own nationals, and this was sufficient to decide the case.

Recommendations for deportation

The above provisions, in particular Council Directive (EEC) 64/ 221, have practical effects in proceedings before British courts. Article 9 of this Directive stipulates that, where there is no right of appeal to a court of law, or where such appeal may only be in respect of the legal validity of the decision, a decision ordering the expulsion of the holder of a residence permit from a territory shall not be taken, until an opinion has been obtained from a competent authority of the host country before which the person concerned enjoys such rights of defence as the domestic law of the country provides. The United Kingdom has not enacted any legislation to take account of this requirement. The position under English law is that a court before whom a person is convicted of an offence has the power to recommend deportation. This has the effect of depriving the defendant of any appeal to the Immigration Appeal Tribunal. The guidelines on sentencing set out in *R* v. *Nazari* (1980) 71 Cr App R 87, [1980] 1 WLR 1366 apply both to those who are nationals of Member States and those who are not.

In Case 131/79 *Santillo* [1980] ECR 1585, [1980] 2 CMLR 308 the Court of Justice ruled that a recommendation by the court is an 'opinion' within article 9 of Directive 64/221. The opinion must, however, be sufficiently proximate in time to the decision ordering expulsion to provide an assurance that there are no new factors to be taken into consideration; and the lapse of several years, as may happen in the case of a person sentenced to imprisonment, is liable to deprive the recommendation of its function as an opinion. In *R* v. *Secretary of State for the Home Department ex parte Santillo* (1981) 73 Cr App R 71 Lord Donaldson said that no court should make an order recommending deportation without full enquiry into the circumstances and should give reasons for its decisions if a recommend-ation is to be made. In *R* v. *Secretary of State for the Home Department ex parte Dannenberg* [1984] QB 766, [1984] 2 WLR 855 the Court of Appeal quashed a deportation order because no reasons were given by the justices, or the Secretary of State, and the failure to give reasons was a breach of Council Directive 64/221.

In *R* v. *Escauriaza* [1989] 3 CMLR 281, 87 Cr App R 344 the Court of Appeal has said that the public policy requirements of Com-munity law are simply mirrored by the law and practice of Eng-land. The requirement that there should be a threat to one of the fundamental interests of society was said simply to mean that the presence of the appellant was to the detriment of the United Kingdom. Whether the European Court would agree that mere detriment is a sufficient definition of the requirements of public policy has yet to be tested.

Non–workers

Three directives on the right of residence for students, retired persons and other members of the non–working population came into effect on 1 July 1992 as part of the programme to establish the single market. Member States are required, under Council Direc-tive 90/364 (EEC) (OJ L180 13.7.90 p26), to grant a right of residence to nationals of Member States who do not enjoy this right under other provisions of Community law. Under Council Directive (EEC) 90/366 (OJ L180 28.7.90 p30) a student can stay for the duration of his course and, under Council Directive 90/365 (EEC) (OJ L180 13.11.90 p28), a person who has retired and is in receipt of a pension can stay in any Member State. These rights are all made subject to a condition not to become a burden on the social security system of the host state. Spouses and dependant relatives, irres-pective of nationality, are entitled to install themselves with the holder of the right of residence.

Council Directive 90/365, unlike Council Regulation 1251/70 (above) that allows a worker to remain in a Member State after he has retired, does not require a retired worker to have exercised a Community right of free movement before his retirement.

Tourists and priests

It appears from Cases 286/82 & 26/83 *Luisi and Carbone* v. *Ministero*

del Tesoro [1984] ECR 377, [1985] 3 CMLR 52 that tourists come
within the category of recipients of services and thus would thus be
protected by Council Directive 64/221 (above). The Court said that
the freedom to provide services includes the freedom for the recipients of services to go to another Member State in order to
receive a service there, and that tourists, persons receiving medical
treatment, and persons travelling for the purpose of education or
business are to be regarded as recipients of services.

An interesting problem is whether a member of a religious order
can be said to be a provider or recipient of services. In Case 196/87
Steymann v. *Staatssecretaris van Justitie* [1989] 1 CMLR 449, the
Advocate General relied upon the Luisi and Carbone case in his
opinion. The Court decided that participation in a community
based on religion is within the Community law on free movement,
but only to the extent that it can be regarded as economic activity.
Hermits and contemplatives might do better to rely on Council
Directive (EEC) 90/364 (above).

Nationality

The right to free movement applies to nationals of Member States.
The United Kingdom has made a declaration (OJ C 23 28.1.83 p1)
with regard to the meaning of the term 'national'. The United
Kingdom regards as nationals, for Community purposes, the following: British citizens; persons who are British subjects by virtue
of Part IV of the British Nationality Act 1981 and so have a right of
abode; and British Dependent Territories citizens who acquired
their citizenship from connection with Gibraltar. The sovereign
base area of Cyprus therefore does not benefit from any of the free
movement provisions, neither does Hong Kong.

Asylum and border control

The view of the Commission, as expressed in the White Paper on
Completing the Internal Market, is that there should be an abolition
of all police and customs formalities for people crossing intra-
community borders. Since this will make it easier for illegal
entrants from outside the Community to cross borders within it,
there is a need for a common policy on immigration. The Maastricht Treaty therefore contains a title concerned with cooperation
in justice and home affairs. Under article K.1 of Title VI Member

States will regard, *inter alia*, asylum policy, rules governing the crossing by persons of the external borders of the Community, immigration policy combatting drug addiction and combatting international fraud as matters of common interest for the purposes of achieving the objectives of the European Union. This is likely to result in the making of conventions under article K.3.

In the light of articles K.1 and K.3, the Conference at Maastricht set their hands to a declaration that they would consider their asylum policies with the aim of harmonizing aspects of them by the beginning of 1993. The process of harmonization had really begun before this declaration with the signing of the Convention Determining the State Responsible for Examining Applications for Asylum Lodged in One of the Member States of the European Communities, commonly known as the Dublin Convention, on 15 June 1990. The object of this convention is to avoid the unseemly spectacle of orbiting refugees. It requires applications for asylum to be examined by one Member State. The pecking order begins with the state where the applicant's family is legally resident, and is followed, respectively, by: the state where he has a valid residence permit or visa; when it can be proved that he has irregularly crossed a border from outside the EC, the state so entered; the state responsible for controlling his entry into the territory of the Member States; and, finally, the first Member State with whom the application is lodged. The United Kingdom gets off lightly because refugees have to swim or use parachutes. In *R* v. *Secretary of State ex parte Mehmet Colak, The Times* 6 July 93, a Turkish Kurd asked for political asylum in the United Kingdom, having travelled via Paris, where he spent four hours in a transit lounge. The Home Office said that, in accordance with the Dublin Convention, he should have his claim considered in Paris, which was the first country he went to after leaving Turkey. On an application for judicial review, Mehmet Colak contended that, as a result of the single market without frontiers established by article 7a of the EC Treaty, there was no power to return him from one Member State to another. However, the court held that article 7a did not bar the Secretary of State from returning him to France. So much for Europe without frontiers.

Chapter 11

Freedom of Establishment and Provision of Services

Article 52 of the EC Treaty confers on the self-employed the right to establish themselves in other Member States. This freedom of establishment includes the right not only to take up and pursue activities as self-employed persons, but also to set up and manage undertakings, companies and firms.

Article 57 is an important corollary to this, in that it provides for the issue of directives for the mutual recognition of formal qualifications. Article 58 states that companies or firms formed in accordance with the law of a Member State, and having their registered office, central administration, or principal place of business within the Community, shall, for the purposes of the provisions on freedom of establishment, be treated in the same way as natural persons who are nationals of Member States.

Freedom to provide services is dealt with separately in articles 59 to 66. With regard both to freedom of establishment and the right to provide services the Treaty provides for a general programme for the abolition of existing restrictions on freedom of movement.

Article 55 derogates from the provisions on freedom of establishment in respect of activities which are connected with the exercise of official authority in the host state. Transport services are governed by the separate title in the Treaty which deals with that activity.

In this chapter we shall examine the rules on freedom of establishment, as they apply to both individuals and companies. The directives on freedom of establishment are published in a publication available from the Office of Official Publications of the European Community or HMSO: *A Guide to Working in a Europe Without Frontiers* by Jean–Claude Séché, ISBN 92–825–8067–9.

The establishment directives

For several occupations secondary legislation has been made in the shape of directives aimed at facilitating the right of establishment and, where applicable, the freedom to provide services. For example, there is a directive relating to hairdressers: Council Directive (EEC) 82/489 (OJ L218 27.7.82 p24). This provides that where the pursuit of hairdressing is subject to the possession of general, commercial, and professional knowledge and ability, Member States are to accept as sufficient evidence of such knowledge that the activity has been pursued lawfully in another Member State for certain specified periods (usually about six years). Proof of the possession of such experience is provided by a certificate issued by the competent authority in the state of origin.

Directives of a more elaborate kind cover architects, doctors, dentists, midwives, and some other professions. For the most part, however, progress has been slow. This has prompted the Commission to introduce a horizontal directive on the recognition of qualifications, Council Directive 89/48 (OJ L19 24.1.89 p46), which has made a considerable impact, not least upon the legal profession. The implementing legislation is the European Communities (Recognition of Professional Qualifications) Regulations 1991, SI 91/824.

This directive is described, in its full title, as a general system for the recognition of higher education diplomas awarded on completion of professional education and training of at least three years' duration. The series of directives which apply to the medical profession make specific provision for the mutual recognition of qualifications throughout the Community, but in most other professions there are no particular directives, and therefore it is necessary to refer to this general directive. The directive applies when a national of a Member State applies to pursue his profession in another Member State. If he holds a diploma from a Member State, he is entitled to pursue his profession anywhere in the Community on the same terms as those which apply to nationals of the host state. The problem which arises when the laws of one Member State insist upon a diploma, but the laws of another do not, is dealt with by a requirement that the applicant should have pursued his profession, full time, for two years, and should possess evidence of one or more formal qualifications. Member States can require applicants to undergo an adaptation period, or take an aptitude test; it is for the applicant to decide which.

There is, however, a derogation from the principle that the applicant can choose whether to take a test, or undergo an adaptation period. In the case of those professions 'whose practice requires precise knowledge of national law and in respect of which the provisions of advice and/or assistance concerning national law is an essential and constant aspect of the professional activity' the host Member State may stipulate either an adaptation period, or an aptitude test. Where the host state proposes to introduce derogations for other professions, as regards an applicant's right to choose, it has to notify the Commission so as to enable other Member States to comment on the proposal.

For EC lawyers who wish to become solicitors the Law Society has devised an aptitude test which consists of two three-hour papers on property and litigation, a two-hour paper on professional conduct and accounts, and an oral test on the principles of common law. Candidates have to demonstrate such a knowledge of English as is necessary for the pursuit of the profession of solicitor in England and Wales.

As for the Bar, an aptitude test has been devised which consists of a four-hour paper on contract, tort, and property, a three-hour paper on the English legal system, a three-hour paper on evidence, and an oral assessment in which the candidate is required to conduct an exercise in advocacy and answer questions on the rules of professional conduct.

Flushed with the success of Directive 89/48, the Council has made a directive for a second general system for the recognition of professional education and training to complement the first. Council Directive 92/51 (OJ L209 24.7.92 p25) covers levels of education and training not covered by the earlier directive, such as those for artificial limb makers and probation officers. Where the taking up of a profession regulated by Council Directive 92/51 is subject to the possession of a diploma, the host state cannot refuse to allow a national of a Member State to take up his occupation on the same conditions as those that apply to its own nationals.

Lawyers in the Community

At the moment the directives for lawyers wishing to practise in the Community are not as comprehensive as those for hairdressers. Save for the general directive on the mutual recognition of diplomas, the only directive to help lawyers is Council Directive (EEC) 77/249 (OJ No L78 26.3.77 p17) which concerns solely the provision of services. There is nothing in it which relates to the establishment of an office in another Member State. It stipulates that a lawyer providing services in another Member State shall adopt the professional title used in the Member State from which he comes. Activities relating to the representation of a client in legal proceedings have to be pursued under the conditions laid down for lawyers established in the host state, with the exception of any conditions requiring residence, or registration with a professional organisation in that state. With regard to representation of a client in litigation, Member States may require lawyers to work in conjunction with a lawyer who practises before the national court.

In the United Kingdom the European Communities (Services of Lawyers) Order 1978 (SI 1978 No 1910) implements the directive. It states that a lawyer from another Member State can provide any service, including appearing before a court, provided that he is instructed along with a United Kingdom advocate, barrister or solicitor. A lawyer from outside the United Kingdom has to decide which role he wishes to play, be it barrister, advocate, or solicitor, for the purposes of the proceedings. If he is instructed with a solicitor he cannot provide the services of a barrister, and *vice versa*. Likewise, a salaried lawyer, acting with a barrister or advocate in proceedings, can provide services only to the extent that a barrister, or advocate, in employment can do so. A lawyer from another Member State cannot engage in conveyancing or probate work, but there are no other restrictions on non-contentious work. A competent authority (the Law Society or the Bar Council) can request him to verify his status as a Community lawyer.

Article 4 of Directive 77/249 requires that a Community lawyer should observe the rules of professional conduct of the host state. This is without prejudice to his duty to observe the rules of conduct prevailing in his own Member State. It puts him in double jeopardy. Those contemplating forays onto the continent had best remember this. It is true that the rule for non-contentious work is modified, to some extent, because article 4(4) speaks only of 'respect for the rules ... which govern the profession in the host Member State'; but the rules on professional secrecy, conflict of interest, publicity and privilege may be entirely different in another Member State. It becomes second nature for a common lawyer to write 'without prejudice' at the head of a letter: remember that these words may not mean anything elsewhere in Europe. A new Common Code of Conduct (see below) seeks to resolve the problems caused by inconsistent professional rules.

In the United Kingdom complaints concerning the conduct of Community lawyers can be made to the Law Society, Bar Council, or equivalent bodies in Scotland and Northern Ireland. The Community lawyer has rights, in disciplinary proceedings, equivalent to those of a United Kingdom lawyer; the disciplinary authority concerned, if it upholds the complaint, must report its finding to the Community lawyer's own professional authority, and may limit his right to provide services in the United Kingdom.

The Common Code of Conduct

The Comité Consultatif des Barreaux Européens (CCBE) is the liaison body in the European Community for the legal professions in the Member States. To this body has been delegated the task of formulating a directive relating to establishment for the legal profession; it has conspicuously failed in that endeavour, although in April 1990 a group of experts did manage to produce a draft proposal for submission to the Commission.

In 1977 the Committee formulated the Declaration of Perugia on the principles of professional conduct of the bars and law societies of the European Community. This does not amount to a code of professional conduct, but it is a statement of common principles. It also contains a little practical advice: 'In some Community countries, all communications between lawyers are regarded as being confidential. This principle is recognized in Belgium, France, Italy, Luxembourg and the Netherlands. The law of the other countries does not accept this as a general principle ... In order to avoid any possibility of misunderstanding which might arise from the disclosure of something said in confidence, the Consultative Committee considers it prudent that a lawyer who wishes to communicate something in confidence to a colleague ... should ask beforehand whether and to what extent his colleague is able to treat it as such.'

In 1988 a Common Code of Conduct was adopted at Strasbourg. The full text was published in the Law Society's *Gazette* on 28 June 1989. A major purpose of the new code is to minimize the problems which may arise from double deontology; that is to say, the application of more than one set of national professional rules of conduct to a particular situation. The problem concerning communications between lawyers of different Member States is met somewhat by article 5 of the Code. This states that if a lawyer sending a communication to another lawyer in another Member State wishes it to remain confidential or without prejudice, he should clearly express this intention when communicating the document. If the recipient is unable to ensure its status as confidential, he should return it to the sender without revealing its contents. The explanatory memorandum which is appended to the code contains a useful summary of the different national rules on confidentiality as they apply in each of the Member States. The European Court recognized the principle of confidentiality in Case 155/79 *A M & S Ltd* v. *EC Commission* [1982] ECR 1575, [1983] QB 878, and the principle is now enshrined in article 2 of the Code.

The Code applies to cross-border activities only. Its provisions include articles relating to the independence of the profession, confidentiality, client funds, insurance, fee sharing and contingency fees. The Code reflects the position in all Member States that unregulated agreements for contingency fees are regarded as contrary to the proper administration of justice.

Professional rules

The Common Code of Conduct was incorporated into the Code of Conduct of the Bar of England and Wales (Annex L) on 31 March 1990 and, since 1 September 1990, it has formed part of both the Solicitors Practice Rules 1990 (Rule 16) and the Solicitors' Overseas Practice Rules 1990 (Rule 4).

The Solicitors Overseas Practice Rules 1990 allow solicitors to be in partnership outside England and Wales with lawyers of other jurisdictions, but such a partnership may only practise in England and Wales, or hold itself out as so practising, if all the non–solicitor partners are on the register of foreign lawyers that the Law Society now has to maintain under section 89 of the Courts and Legal Services Act 1990. The way was made open for multi–national practices by section 66 of that act, and such arrangements are now permitted by amendments to the Solicitors Practice Rules made by the Multi–National Legal Practice Rules 1991. When such a partnership practises in England the foreign lawyer is required to register with the Law Society so that clients will receive the same kind of protection that they would receive if a purely English firm were instructed; detailed rules, including, for example, an obligation for the foreign lawyer to contribute to the Law Society's compensation fund, are set out in Schedule 14 of the Act.

The Overseas Practice Rules of the English Bar are set out in Annex F of the Bar Code of Conduct. A barrister, subject to minor reservations, may take instructions from a foreign lawyer which do not relate to conveyancing, litigation already begun in the United Kingdom, or the drafting of documents instituting proceedings. A barrister can also accept instructions direct from any lay client in relation to matters which are mainly foreign in content. In international arbitration proceedings the rules are even more relaxed.

A barrister can accept instructions direct from a lay client for work relating to foreign matters to be performed abroad; or, even if the work is not going to be done abroad, relating to foreign litigation or subsidiary to work done abroad. A lay client who carries on business abroad or usually lives outside the United Kingdom can (subject to the same restrictions as apply to foreign lawyers) instruct a barrister direct, provided that a solicitor has not already instructed the barrister and that the instructions emanate from abroad. A barrister can employ anyone outside the United Kingdom who is not a solicitor practising in England and Wales and can enter into a partnership with a solicitor provided that the latter does not practise in the United Kingdom.

Clearly there are cost advantages to Community lawyers and their clients who take advantage of these rules. They are, however, somewhat bizarre when seen in the light of Directive 77/249. The latter does not apply between the component parts of the United Kingdom. Community lawyers, for example, are actually better off than English lawyers with regard to practice in Scotland; under section 60 of the Courts and Legal Services Act, and section 30 of the Law Reform (Miscellaneous Provisions) (Scotland) Act 1990, however, the Lord Chancellor is given powers to make regulations to cure this anomaly.

Annexes I and K of the Bar Code of Conduct allow foreign lawyers to practise from chambers in England, and require barristers with dual qualifications to follow the rules for foreign lawyers practising from English chambers in respect of their foreign practices.

Lawyers in France

In France there has been resistance to implementing Directive 77/249. In Case 294/89 *Commission* v. *France* [1991] ECR I–3591 the Commission brought an action against France for its failure to implement Directive 77/249. The French were castigated for *inter alia* requiring foreign lawyers to act in conjunction with a member of the French Bar even when acting in situation where French law does not require the compulsory assistance of a lawyer.

The judgment has been helpful to lawyers wishing to practise in France, but the real difficulty is that there is no establishment directive that would form a proper basis for the activities of European practitioners. Whereas in the United Kingdom there is no objection to a foreign lawyer dispensing his wares without interference from the local profession, the view of the French Republic is that no lawyer should be trusted to practise who is not a member of the local legal profession. Recent reforms have merged the profession of *conseil juridique* with that of *avocat*. Some foreign lawyers in France who were already members of the *conseil juridique* profession automatically became *avocats*, others, who were established in France for a period, have been permitted to become *avocats* as well. But, for the future, the intention is that all lawyers must qualify under the French system.

The French *Avocats* Decree 1991 (November 27), the main legislation implementing the reforms, was made after the judgment in the above case. It contains rules governing the admission of EC nationals to the French profession, and implements Directive 77/ 249 by setting out a list of professions in other Member States whose members are to be regarded as equivalent to *avocats* for the purposes of the directive. A foreign *avocat* must present himself for verification of his qualifications before the appropriate local bar before he is free to practise; when practising in France he is expected to obey the same disciplinary rules as his French counterpart.

Gullung

Case 292/86 *Gullung* v. *Conseil de l'Ordre des Avocats du Barreau de Colmar* [1988] ECR 111, [1988] 2 CMLR 57 is one of the few cases which have presented the European Court with the opportunity to clarify the position of Community lawyers wishing to establish themselves in another Member State. Mr Gullung was a national both of France and Germany. Because of disciplinary measures taken against him he resigned from practice in France. He then succeeded in being admitted to the German Bar as a Rechtsanwalt. He had his main office at Kehl in Germany. He tried to set up an office just across the border in France, holding himself out as 'jurisconsulte', but the Mulhouse Bar resolved that its members would refuse to lend him any assistance. The affair found its way to the European Court which, amongst other questions, was asked whether a lawyer, who is a national of a Member State, is entitled to establish himself elsewhere in the Community. Because there was no directive dealing with the right of establishment Mr Gullung relied on the direct effect of article 52 of the Treaty. The Court, however, confined itself to the question of a lawyer who uses the title used by lawyers in the host state. In such a case, in the absence of any implementing directive, the host state was entitled to impose an obligation to enrol with the local bar. Despite a request by the British Government for clarification of the position of a lawyer who simply uses his home title, the Court found it unnecessary to go further. *Gullung* is, therefore, a somewhat unsatisfactory case. One can only hope that before long an issue will arise where the Court has to address itself directly to the issue of establishment.

Clearly the task of integrating the European legal profession is not an easy one. But, at the time of writing the Commission was considering a new draft for an establishment directive which may come into force soon.

Chapter 12

Competition

Article 3(g) of the EC Treaty states that the activities of the Community include a system ensuring that competition in the internal market is not distorted. The fundamental rules on competition are contained in articles 85 and 86 of the Treaty. These rules apply to any enterprise trading directly or indirectly in the Community, no matter where it is established; Japanese or US companies are, therefore, as much affected as Community enterprises. Article 85(1) of the Treaty prohibits agreements which may affect trade between Member States, and article 85(2) declares contracts containing such restrictions void; although, if the restrictive terms are severable, only the severable parts are void.

Article 85(3) of the Treaty gives the Commission the power to exempt practices which have certain redeeming beneficial effects. As well as making application to the Commission for exemption, companies may sometimes need to check with the Commission in order to reassure themselves that their agreements do not offend against the competition rules: the latter procedure is known as an application for 'negative clearance'. EC Council Regulation No 17 (OJ 13 21.2.62 p204, Sp edn 1959–62 p87) sets out the procedure by which applications are made to the Commission both for negative clearance and exemption under article 85.

The Treaty provisions

The Treaty rules are so important that they had best be set out in full:

Rules Applying to Undertakings

Article 85. 1. The following shall be prohibited as incompatible with the common market: all agreements between undertakings, decisions by associations of undertakings and concerted practices which may affect trade between Member States and which have as their object or effect the prevention restriction or distortion of competition within the common market, and in particular those which:

(a) directly or indirectly fix purchase or selling prices or any other trading conditions;
(b) limit or control production, markets, technical development, or investment;
(c) share markets or sources of supply;
(d) apply dissimilar conditions to equivalent transactions with other trading parties, thereby placing them at a competitive disadvantage;
(e) make the conclusion of contracts subject to acceptance by other parties of supplementary obligations which, by their nature or according to commercial usage, have no connection with the subject matter of such contracts.

2. Any agreements or decisions prohibited pursuant to this Article shall be automatically void.

3. The provisions of Paragraph 1 may, however, be declared inapplicable in the case of:

- any agreement or category of agreement between under-takings;
- any decisions or category of decisions by associations of undertakings;
- any concerted practice or category of concerted practices;

which contributes to improving the production or distribution of goods or to promoting technical or economic progress, while allowing consumers a fair share of the resulting benefit, and which does not:

(a) impose on the undertakings concerned restrictions which are not indispensable to the attainment of these objectives;
(b) afford such undertakings the possibility of eliminating com-petition in respect of a substantial part of the products in question.

Article 86. Any abuse by one or more undertakings of a dominant position within the common market or in a substantial part of it shall be prohibited as incompatible with the common market in so far as it may affect trade between the Member States.
  Such abuse may, in particular, consist in:

(a) directly or indirectly imposing unfair purchase or selling prices or other unfair trading conditions;

(b) limiting production, markets or technical development to the prejudice of consumers;
(c) applying dissimilar conditions to equivalent transactions with other trading parties, thereby placing them at a competitive disadvantage;
(d) making the conclusion of contracts subject to the acceptance by the other parties of supplementary obligations which, by their nature or according to commercial usage, have no connection with the subject of such contracts.

Application of article 85

Agreements falling within article 85(1) are automatically void. The scope of such a prohibition is wide. It can extend to 'horizontal' agreements such as cartels, market sharing, and price fixing between supplier and supplier. It also extends, with rather less justification, to 'vertical' agreements such as distribution, licensing, and exclusive purchasing agreements between different levels in the trade. The European Court has shown, however, that it is prepared to accept that sometimes a degree of market protection is necessary before a distributor can be expected to take the risk of entering the market at all.

In the Maize Seeds case, Case 258/78 *Nungesser* v. *Commission* [1982] ECR 2105, [1983] 1 CMLR 278, there was a licensing agreement for the exploitation of some plant breeders' rights that the Commission contended was contrary to article 85(1). The Court held that the agreement was permissible, since otherwise there would be no incentive for anyone to risk introducing novel crop varieties onto the market. When the Court adopts such reasoning it is sometimes said to apply a 'rule of reason', and the test it applies is whether the terms in question are really necessary to secure access to the market. The Court went so far as to allow of a clause which conferred on the plaintiffs an exclusive territory, and protected them from competition from the owners of the plant breeder's rights. However, the judgment made clear that an exclusive licence, with absolute territorial protection, which would eliminate competition from third parties and cut out parallel imports, would go far beyond what was necessary for the improvement of production or distribution or the promotion of technical progress.

Only those parts of the agreement which are incompatible with article 85 are affected. The consequence of this nullity for other parts of the agreement is no concern of Community law. The way in which the English courts will apply this blue pencil test is not quite clear. In *Chemidus Wavin Ltd* v. *Société pour la Transformation et l'Exploitation des Résines Industrielles SA* [1978] 3 CMLR 514 the Court of Appeal doubted whether it was really a question of severance in the way the English courts use that term in considering whether covenants are void as being in restraint of trade, and, if they are to any extent void, whether those covenants can be severed so as to save part of the covenant, although another part may be bad. Buckley LJ said that one may have to consider whether, after the excisions required by article 85, the contract could be said to fail for lack of consideration, or might have so changed its character as not to be the sort of contract that the parties intended to enter into at all.

An agreement or practice must be one which may affect trade between Member States before it is subject to article 85. In Case 56/65 *Société Technique Minière* v. *Maschinenbau Ulm GmbH* [1966] ECR 235, [1966] CMLR 357 it was said that this means that it must be possible to foresee, with a sufficient degree of probability, on the basis of a set of objective factors of law or fact, that the agreement in question may have an influence on the pattern of trade between Member States. The influence may be direct or indirect, actual or potential.

An agreement extending over the whole of the territory of a Member State, by its very nature, has the effect of reinforcing the compartmentalization of the market on a national basis. Case 8/72 *Cementhandelaren* v. *Commission* [1972] ECR 977, [1973] CMLR 7 arose out of a number of decisions made by the Netherlands Cement Dealers Association. The trade in cement in the Netherlands was regulated not by agreement, but by the decisions of this association. The Association introduced a purely national cartel whereby the price of cement was fixed, for sales of less than 100 tonnes and, for larger sales, a target price applied. The Court said that this arrangement would hold up the economic interpenetration which the Treaty was designed to bring about, and thus offended article 85.

The kinds of agreements affected by article 85 are not confined to contracts in the legal sense. In Case 41/69 *ACF Chemiefarma NV* v. *EC Commission* [1970] ECR 661 several companies entered into an agreement fixing prices and quotas for the export of quinine. A gentlemen's agreement extended its provisions to all sales within the Common Market. It was held that a gentlemen's agreement, if it contains clauses restricting competition in the Common Market, may fall under the prohibition contained in article 85(1).

Article 85 extends to concerted practices. A concerted practice, sometimes called 'concertation', does not have all the elements of a contract, but may arise out of coordination which becomes apparent from the behaviour of the participants. Of course, the companies concerned will excuse themselves by saying that there is no collusion; everyone just happens to be charging the same price. In the *Dyestuffs* case, Case 48/69 *Imperial Chemicals Limited* v. *EC Commission* [1972] ECR 619, [1972] CMLR 557, the meaning of 'concerted practices' was discussed. It was said that article 85 distinguishes the concept of concerted practices from that of agreements between enterprises in order to bring under the prohibition of article 85 a form of co-ordination between undertakings which, without going so far as to amount to an agreement properly so called, knowingly substitutes a practical cooperation between them for the risks of competition. Although parallel behaviour may not, by itself, amount to a concerted practice, it may be strong evidence of such a practice, if it leads to conditions of competition which do not correspond to normal conditions.

The facts of the *Dyestuffs* case were quite striking. From January 1964 to October 1967 three general and uniform increases in the prices of dyestuffs took place in the Community. ICI argued that this extraordinary coincidence was the result of 'price leadership' by one undertaking. It was said that such a situation would arise where there was an oligopoly, that is to say a market which consists of a small number of large firms. In its grounds of judgment the Court said that if parallel conduct is such as to enable those concerned to attempt to stabilize prices at a level different from that to which competition would have led, and to consolidate established positions, to the detriment of effective freedom of movement of products in the Common Market, it was particularly strong evidence of a concerted practice.

At the time this case arose the United Kingdom was not a member of the Community, so the case is also interesting from the point of view of the attitude of the Court to the position of subsidiaries established within the Community. It was said that by making use of its subsidiaries in the Community ICI was able to ensure that its decisions were implemented on the market. The fact that a subsidiary has separate legal personality is not sufficient to exclude the possibility of imputing its conduct to the parent company. Such may be the case particularly where the subsidiary, although having separate legal personality, does not decide independently upon its own conduct on the market but carries out, in all material respects, the instructions given to it by the parent company. Where a subsidiary does not enjoy real autonomy in determining its course of action in the market, the prohibitions set out in article 85(1) may be considered inapplicable in the relationship between it and the parent company with which it forms one economic unit. In view of the unity of the group thus formed, the actions of the subsidiaries may in certain circumstances be attributed to the parent company. The *Dyestuffs* case contains the first mention of a principle, now established, that an undertaking is an entity which may include a parent company and its subsidiaries.

ICI contended that, because it was a company from outside the Community, there was no jurisdiction. The Court rejected that argument; an agreement does not have to be made within the Community, or even between Community companies, for its effects to be felt within the Community. The European Court justifies its jurisdiction in such cases by means of this reasoning, known as the 'effects doctrine'.

The *Dyestuffs* case can be contrasted with the recent Wood Pulp case, Case 89/85 *A Ahlstrom Osakeyhtio and others* v. *Commission* (31 March 1993 *transcript*), in which the Commission asserted that certain producers of wood pulp had concerted on their prices by means of a system of quarterly price announcements. The European Court held that conduct could not in itself amount to concertation. There was communication between producers because of periodic price announcements, but these announcements did not lessen each undertaking's uncertainty about what others would do; therefore concertation was not the only plausible explanation for their parallel conduct. 'Concertation' is a new-fangled word for concerted practices.

Case 15/74 *Centrafarm BV* v. *Sterling Drug Inc.* [1974] ECR 1147, [1974] 2 CMLR 480 is a case where there was an arrangement between the proprietor of parallel patents in various Member States and his licensees. It clarifies the principle that article 85 has no place in collusion between a parent and its subsidiary company, if they both form one economic unit where the subsidiary has no freedom and the collusive conduct has to do with the internal allocation of tasks between the undertakings.

Article 85 contains no definition of 'undertaking'. The term seems to be left deliberately vague; it appears to include undertakings in the economic or commercial sense. Defined in this way even an individual may be an undertaking. Commission Decision (EEC) 76/743 *Re Reuter/BASF AG* [1976] 2 CMLR D44 (OJ L254 17.9.76 p10) arose because of a complaint by Dr Reuter, a research chemist, who held shares in a group of companies. He complained about a non-competition clause which had been imposed on him. It was part of a contract made when a group of companies controlled by him had been sold. The Commission regarded Dr Reuter as an undertaking because he engaged in economic activity through the group of firms which remained under his control and by exploiting the results of his own research.

The reference, in article 85, to decisions by associations of undertakings is designed to include decisions by trade associations, as happened in the Cementhandelaren case. In the United Kingdom a series of agreements and decisions by the Publishers Association and its members had the effect of restricting the market in books, and controlling their retail prices. This arrangement was known as the Net Book Agreement; it was notified to the Commission soon after the United Kingdom joined the Community, but remained valid until the Commission had time to consider it because it was an 'old agreement', that is to say one which was in existence before article 85 was brought into effect. It was not until 1989 that the Commission decided to prohibit it, by Commission Decision (EEC) 89/44 (OJ L22 26.1.89 p12). The publishers made an application for exemption under the provisions of article 85(3) of the Treaty; it was refused. Pending the outcome of annulment proceedings the European Court was persuaded to suspend the operation of the decision, but ultimately the case came on for hearing before the Court of First Instance.

It was argued that the issues had already been decided by the Restrictive Practices Court in the United Kingdom in 1962, but the Court of First Instance said that a Commission decision cannot be vitiated on the ground that it did not specifically rebut the previous findings of a national court, that the Commission had considered the 1962 judgment, and that in any event national judicial practices cannot prevail in the application of the EC competition rules: Case T–66/89 *Publishers Association* v. *EC Commission* [1992] 5 CMLR 120.

Agreements which have as their 'object or effect' the distortion of competition fall within the terms of article 85. Several examples of such agreements are give in sub-paragraphs (a) to (e) of article 85(1). The list is not exhaustive, but it does indicate the sorts of agreements which require careful consideration. One should be careful when drafting or construing, *inter alia*, the following: price fixing agreements, market sharing arrangements, distribution agreements, patent licences, know–how licences, agreements fixing discounts or other trading conditions and differentiating them according to the particular distributor or customer, agreements preventing parallel imports, and export bans.

The requirements that an agreement should have as its 'object or effect' the prevention restriction or distortion of competition are to be read disjunctively. In Case 56/65 *Société Technique Minière* v. *Maschinenbau Ulm GmbH* [1966] ECR 235, [1966] CMLR 357 the Court explained that those requirements are not cumulative but alternative. It found that it was necessary to consider the precise purpose of the agreement, in the economic context in which it is applied. But, if that analysis failed to reveal a sufficiently deleterious effect on competition, the consequences of the agreement should also be considered.

Cases 56 and 58/64 *Consten SARL and Grundig Verkaufs* v. *EEC Commission* [1966] ECR 299, [1966] CMLR 418 arose out of an agreement whereby Consten were granted sole distribution rights in France for the products of Grundig. It was said that, for the purposes of the application of article 85(1), there was no need to take account of the concrete effects of the agreement when it has as its object the prevention, restriction or distortion of competition. The *Consten* case is, by the way, a leading case in the entire area of competition, and is useful not only with regard to the substantive law in this area, but also its procedural aspects.

Special sectors

The basic principle is that the competition rules apply to all sectors of the economy, but agriculture is treated as a special case, and transport has its own detailed rules. Coal and steel are not covered by the competition rules because of article 232 of the EC Treaty which states that provisions of the ECSC Treaty are not affected.

Article 42 of the EC Treaty states that the Treaty articles relating to competition apply to the production and trade in agricultural products only to the extent determined by the Council. Council Regulation (EEC) 26/62 (OJ 30 20.4.62 p993, Sp edn 1959–62 p129) has applied the competition rules to production and trade in agricultural products, but not where the agreement forms part of a national market organization. Nearly all agricultural products are subject to such a market organization.

Transport was originally included within the purview of Regulation 17, but was promptly exempted by Council Regulation 141/62 (OJ 124 28.11.62 p2751, Sp edn 1959–62 p291). In 1968, however, it was brought back into the fold by Council Regulation 1017/68 (OJ L175 23.7.68 p1, Sp edn 1968 (I) p302) which applies the rules of competition to transport by rail, road, and inland transport. Maritime transport was made subject to detailed rules by Council Regulation (EEC) 4056/86 (OJ L378 31.12.86 p4). Air transport between Member States has been made subject to detailed rules by Council Regulation (EEC) 3975/87 (OJ L374 31.12.87 p1); but this regulation applies only to air transport between Community airports.

Where there are no detailed rules on competition article 85 of the Treaty is not directly applicable. This is because, until the entry into force of implementing directives, the transitional rules of articles 88 and 89 of the Treaty apply. Under these transitional rules it is for Member States to rule on the application of the competition rules, or for the Commission to record an infringement under article 89. Agreements do not become automatically void under article 85 until the transitional procedure has taken place. The position is discussed in Case 66/86 *Ahmeed Saeed Flugreisen and Silver Line Reisebüro v Zentralezur Bekämpfung Unlauteren Wettbewerbs eV* [1989] ECR 803, [1990] 4 CMLR 102, and Cases 209 to 213/84 *Ministère Public v Asjes* [1986] ECR 1425, [1986] 3 CMLR 173. Because the detailed rules adopted with regard to air transport apply only to flights between Community airports, routes to non–member states are still subject to the transitional rules.

Minor agreements

The Court of Justice has applied a *de minimis* principle; trade must be affected to an appreciable extent before article 85 will apply. In Case 19/77 *Miller International Schallplatten GmbH* v. *Commission* [1978] ECR 131, [1978] 2 CMLR 334 Advocate General Warner said that, in order for this plea to be accepted, 'the breach of article 85(1) must indeed be negligible.' It appears, therefore, that the principle is of limited effect. It may well be that the offending party has a small share of the market in general but if the market is sufficiently defined the share will be greater. Miller International was a producer of records and cassettes. It was true that it had a small share of the market in those goods, but half its repertoire consisted of recordings for children. In the children's market it had a leading position and could not escape the effects of article 85. The Commission takes the view that certain agreements are of minor importance and should not be affected by competition rules. The Commission Notice on Minor Agreements (OJ No C231 12.9.86 p2) indicates that the following conditions have to be fulfilled:

- the goods or services which are the subject of the agreement do not represent more than 5 per cent of the total market for such goods in the area of the Common Market affected by the agreement; and
- the aggregate turnover of the companies involved does not exceed 200 million ECUs.

Tipp-Ex

Commission Decision 87/407, *Tipp-Ex* (OJ 1987 L222 10.8.87 p1) is by no means a remarkable case, but it serves as a useful example of how Community competition law works in practice, and is a salutary example of what can go wrong. Tipp-Ex Vertrieb GmbH & Co KG was described as a company with a strong position in the market for correction paper and fluids, but by no means occupying a dominant position. The proceedings concerned agreements and concerted practices between Tipp-Ex and its exclusive distributors in several Member States.

One of the distributors of Tipp-Ex was a French company, ISA, which bought Tipp-Ex products and then resold them on the German market. In other words, it engaged in parallel importing, thus undercutting other exclusive distributors. Tipp-Ex then brought pressure to bear in order to cut off the parallel market. ISA complained to the Commission.

During the Commission investigation a variety of evidence was unearthed. There was a telex to another distributor which ended with the sentence: 'We hope that you are able to help us to cut out the parallel market'. Another telex addressed to various distributors asked whether it made sense for an exclusive distributor to place his distributorship in jeopardy and stated that action would be taken. Another telex to a company which had delivered supplies to ISA said that: 'Although it is impossible on legal grounds to stop supplies, special prices should no longer apply'.

The system used by Tipp-Ex depended mainly on oral agreements, but, at a later stage, written standard form contracts were drawn up. These contained clauses restricting sales outside the contract territory: 'With regard to EEC Member States not included in the contract territory the Authorized Dealer undertakes not to engage in active sales'. And, there were clauses protecting the contract territory: 'The Supplier shall not supply the contract goods to distributors who to his knowledge intend to resell them in the contract territory'.

It was easy for the Commission to make out a case from the above evidence. Tipp-Ex decided to rely on what amounts to a plea in mitigation. Its first submission was that prior to 1982 it had no knowledge of article 85 of the Treaty. This did not impress the Commission. Its most heart-rending plea was that it had 'instructed a lawyer to draw up a standard form contract with a view to placing its relations on a legally sound basis' and 'relied on the opinion of a lawyer who spent a considerable amount of time dealing with the legal questions involved and charged commensurately high fees'.

Altogether it was a sad case. The Commission found, using a typical phrase, that the conduct of Tipp-Ex and its dealers amounted 'at least to a concerted practice'. It was moved to compassion, however, by the expressed readiness of Tipp-Ex to put its house in order. A fine of 400 000 ECUs, which is very modest by current standards, was imposed.

Exemptions

The Commission has the power to exempt agreements from the effect of article 85(1) of the Treaty. It can declare article 85(1) inapplicable, if the agreement contributes to improving the production or distribution of goods or to promoting technical or economic progress while allowing consumers a fair share of the resulting benefit. Regulation 17 (OJ 13 21.2.62 p204, Sp edn 1959–60 p87) creates a system whereby undertakings can apply to the Commission for exemption.

The purpose of the exemption procedure is to allow undertakings to enter into arrangements that, taken as a whole, offer economic benefits, although they would otherwise be forbidden. A manufacturer might argue, for example, that his distributor should have an exclusive territory in which to promote a new product, as an incentive to sales and a means of increasing competition between different brands. Two manufacturers might wish to come to an agreement which would enable each to specialize in a particular product, instead of both manufacturing the entire range.

If an application for exemption is successful the Commission will make a decision declaring article 85(1) to be inapplicable. Under article 8 of Regulation 17 the exemption is issued for a specified period. In practice this period is unlikely to be longer than about five years. The Commission may revoke or amend its decision or prohibit specific acts by the parties.

It is sometimes difficult to know whether to notify an agreement. By notifying an agreement the company will attract the attention of the Commission, which may be minded to forbid conduct which has hitherto gone unnoticed. If in doubt it is usually best to notify. The Commission can impose fines of up to 10 per cent of turnover on undertakings which intentionally or negligently infringe article 85(1) or article 86. Under article 15 of Regulation 17, however, the fines cannot be imposed in respect of acts taking place after notification to the Commission and before its decision under article 85(3) of the Treaty, provided that they fall within the activity described in the notification. Any party to the agreement can notify it to the Commission.

Block exemptions

In order to obviate the need for the Commission to examine, on an individual basis, many agreements which have the same basic objectives there is a system of 'block exemptions'. The block exemptions are set out in several regulations, each of which exempts a category of agreements from the provisions of article 85(1) of the Treaty.

There are some eight regulations, which relate to the following kinds of agreement: exclusive distribution agreements, Commission Regulation 1983/83 (OJ L173 30.6.83 p1); exclusive purchasing, Commission Regulation 1984/83 (OJ L173 30.6.83 p5); patent licensing, Commission Regulation 2349/84 (OJ L219 16.8.84 p15); motor vehicle distribution and servicing, Commission Regulation 123/85 (OJ L15 18.1.85 p16); 'specialisation agreements', Commission Regulation 417/85 (OJ L 53 22.2.85 p1); research and development agreements, Commission Regulation 418/85 (OJ L53 22.2.85 p5); franchising, Commission Regulation 4087/88 (OJ L359 28.12.88 p46); and, know-how licensing, Commission Regulation 556/89 (OJ L61 4.3.89 p1). 'Specialisation agreements' are reciprocal arrangements where each party agrees with the other not to manufacture certain products so that they can each concentrate on fewer production lines. In addition to the above there are four regulations relating to air transport.

The block exemptions regulations contain lists of terms which are permissible, the so called 'white' clauses, and lists of forbidden terms, the so called 'black clauses'. Some of the regulations take effect automatically without the need for notification to the

Commission. Other regulations contain provisions for an 'opposition procedure'.

The opposition procedure is a process which requires that, in certain cases, the Commission must be notified before the exemption applies. The regulation on patent licensing agreements may be taken as an example. If the licensing agreement contains restrictions on competition that are not listed in the regulation the agreement can still be exempted; but the agreement must be notified to the Commission. The Commission then has six months in which to oppose the exemption. If it raises no objection the exemption will apply.

Negative clearance

The negative clearance procedure allows undertakings to ascertain whether the Commission considers that their arrangements are prohibited under article 85 or 86 of the Treaty. If the application is successful the Commission will make a decision certifying that, on the basis of the facts in its possession, there are no grounds under 85(1) or 86 of the Treaty for action on its part in respect of the arrangements or behaviour. An application for negative clearance will normally be made at the same time, and, indeed, on the same form as an application for exemption.

If the agreement has been drawn in such a way that it clearly falls within one of the block exemptions there will be little point in notifying it to the Commission; unless the company wishes to draw attention to itself.

Abuse of a dominant position

Article 86 of the Treaty differs from article 85 in that it is concerned not with collusive activity but the dominance of undertakings whose position is powerful enough for them to bully others. The leading case in this area is Case 6/72 *Europemballage Corporation and Continental Can Company Inc* v. *EC Commission* [1979] ECR 215, [1973] CMLR 199. The Continental Can Company of New York set up a company called Europemballage which was registered in Delaware. Europemballage then took over a Netherlands company, Thomassen. The arrangement gave Continental Can a powerful position in the European packaging market. The Commission found that, by purchasing 80 per cent of the shares in Thomassen,

Continental Can had infringed article 86, and required the company to put an end to the infringement. Continental Can appealed to the European Court.

The first problem in the Continental Can case was to determine whether article 86 applied at all, because the article would appear to be concerned not with the acquisition of a dominant position, but its abuse. In its grounds of judgment the Court said that abuse may occur if an undertaking in a dominant position so strengthens its position that the degree of dominance reached substantially fetters competition, so that the only undertakings remaining in the market are those whose behaviour depends on the dominant one.

The Court then turned to what became the real issue in the case, namely whether there had been an abuse of dominance in the relevant market. The definition of the relevant market is central to all cases under article 86. In the *Brass Band Instruments* decision (OJ L286 9.10.87 p36), the history of which has already been described (see Chapter 2), the relevant market was the market for brass band instruments. It was fairly easy to define: brass bands cannot easily switch to using pianos and harmonicas. Case 27/76 *United Brands Co v. EC Commission* [1978] ECR 207, [1987] 1 CMLR 429 involved the interesting question whether, in the case of an importer of bananas, the relevant market was soft fruit or bananas. The Commission submitted that there is a demand for bananas which is distinct from the demand for other fresh fruit, especially as the banana is such a very important part of the diet of certain sections of the community. The report of the case occupies some 144 pages, thus demonstrating how much can be said about bananas. It was held that the relevant market is the banana market.

The market is determined by looking at, *inter alia*: 'demand substitutability', that is to say the extent to which other products are available on the market; 'supply substitutability', whether other manufacturers can enter the market; the geographical market; and, the temporal market. Demand substitutability is measured by 'cross-elasticity of demand' which is a function of the ease with which customers will switch to other products if there is a price rise. In the Continental Can case the Commission failed to show that customers could not conveniently switch from the tin cans provided by the plaintiffs to glass containers. The metal closures provided by the plaintiffs were not expensive to transport, so they could easily be shipped in from other manufacturers. Moreover, food canners could easily produce cans themselves if they wished.

Dominance

In the United Brands case (above) dominance was defined as a position of economic strength enjoyed by an undertaking which enables it to hinder the maintenance of effective competition on the relevant market by allowing it to behave to an appreciable extent independently of its competitors and customers, and ultimately of consumers.

Market share does not necessarily indicate that there is a position of dominance. The Commission, however, takes the view that a dominant position is reached where an undertaking has acquired a 40–45 per cent market share.

Abuse

Abuse may be 'exclusionary', such as predatory pricing, loyalty rebates and refusal to supply; or 'exploitative' such as charging unfairly high prices, tying, or imposing unfairly low prices on suppliers. In the *Brass Band Instruments* case the abuse was a refusal to supply. Likewise, in the United Brands case the plaintiff had used its strong position in the market in order to refuse to supply bananas to a distributor. In its decision in *Eurofix/Hilti* (OJ L65 11.3.88 p.19) the Commission found there was an abuse when there was a 'tying' arrangement. Hilti sold nail guns. It pursued a policy of tying the sale of nails to patented cartridge strips so that independent nail manufacturers could not enter the market; it was impossible to get nails except from Hilti. The Continental Can case shows that abuse may consist not merely in unfair trading, but also in changing the very structure of the market. Mere dominance, however, does not amount to an abuse; therefore article 86 is not a satisfactory basis for the control of mergers, and specific regulations have had to be made to deal with that.

Mergers

Because the Continental Can case did not provide a good basis for the development of law on mergers, two regulations were enacted. Council Regulation (EEC) 4064/89 (OJ L395 30.12.89 p1) contains the substantive law on mergers. It applies to all mergers which have a Community dimension. A merger has a Community dimension if *inter alia* the world turnover of the participants is greater than 5000 million ECUs, and the individual turnover within the Community of at least two of the undertakings is more than 250 million ECUs. Undertakings must give prior notice of such mergers. The procedural rules on notifications, time limits, and hearings are set out in Commission Regulation (EEC) 2367/90 (OJ L219 14.8.90 p5).

Regulation 17

Council Regulation 17 (OJ 13 21.2.62 p24, Sp edn 1959-62 p87)) governs not only the procedure with regard to applications for exemption and negative clearance, but also the powers of the Commission to impose fines and conduct investigations into matters relating to competition.

Exemption and negative clearance

The procedure for applying for exemption and negative clearance is time-consuming and tedious. Commission Regulation (EEC) 27/62 (OJ L35 11.5.62 p.118, Sp edn 1959-62 p132) as amended by Commission Regulation (EEC) 2526/85 (OJ L 240 7.9.85 p1) prescribes a form, Form A/B, which must be used when notifying agreements. Thirteen copies are required: one for the Commission and one for each Member State.

An application for negative clearance does not automatically count as an application for exemption, though both applications will usually be made on the same form. The information given on the form is detailed and relates to the market for the goods or services, the structure of the companies involved, details of the proposed arrangements, and the reasons why an application is being made for negative clearance or exemption. Even if the application is only made as a precaution, in order to obtain an exemption the applicant must state how the proposed arrangements are said to improve production or distribution, or promote technical and economic progress.

Complaints

Complaints of infringement of articles 85 or 86 of the Treaty can be made under article 3 of Regulation 17. Those entitled to make an application are Member States and natural or legal persons who can claim a legitimate interest; but the Commission may also act of its own initiative, so those unable to show strictly that they have a legitimate interest can still complain, and hope that the Commission will take up the cudgels on their behalf.

In competition cases the complaint will be, for example, that there is an agreement or cartel which distorts competition in the Community, or that a company has abused a dominant situation in the common market. The Commission has prepared a form, form C, for use when making complaints but a complaint does not have to take any particular form; a letter will do. Form C provides for the complainant to identify the parties, give details of the infringements of the Treaty, show that the complainant has a legitimate interest, annex any evidence and documents relied on, state what steps have been taken to bring the infringement to an end, and declare that the contents are correct.

Comfort letters

In practice exemptions are rare. Negative clearance may be unnecessary where the parties have in fact drafted their agreement with the object of avoiding the effects of article 85, and many problems are dealt with in an informal manner. There is scope for renegotiating the agreement; the Commission may require amendments to be made. More often than not the Commission will send a 'comfort letter' saying that the Commission is closing its file and that there is no reason to take further action; sometimes the letter will say that the agreement merits exemption. The national courts are supposed to take such a letter into account when dealing with competition cases, as was said in Case 99/79 *Lancôme SA v Etos BV* [1980] ECR 2511, [1981] 2 CMLR 164, but a comfort letter does not actually confer any exemption.

Hearings

Article 19 of Regulation 17 provides that the Commission shall give parties an opportunity to be heard before it takes any decision on negative clearance, exemption or fines. The procedure is set out in Commission Regulation (EEC) 99/63 (OJ 127 20.8.63 p.2268, Sp edn 1963–64 p.47).

A company, or it may be an undertaking or association, against whom, for example, a complaint has been made will receive a statement of objections from the Commission which identifies the issues. At the same time the Commission fixes the time limit, usually six or eight weeks, during which the company has an opportunity to reply. The time limit may not be less than two weeks and may be extended. The Commission will usually inform the company of the contents of its file by means of an annex attached to the statement of objections, although certain documents may be withheld on the grounds of confidentiality.

In its reply the company may set out all the matters relevant to its defence and attach any relevant documents in proof of the facts relied on. If it so requests in its written comments, the company is entitled to have an oral hearing before the Commission. The hearing is informal before an official called the Hearing Officer; the public are not admitted but minutes are kept which are read and approved by each person heard. Persons appearing before the Commission may be assisted by lawyers. Third parties may be heard if they have a sufficient interest.

The Hearing Officer does not give a judgment; it is an administrative hearing only. Any decision will be drafted by DG IV (the department of the Commission which deals with competition matters). An appeal against a decision will lie to the Court of First Instance.

Powers of the Commission

In order to carry out its tasks, the first need of the Commission is to acquire information. Under article 11 of Regulation 17 it can request information from companies and other undertakings. If the request is refused, the Commission can proceed by way of a decision to demand information. Under article 15 there is power to impose fines of up to 5000 ECUs where, whether intentionally or negligently, either no information or incorrect information is supplied.

Under article 14(1) the Commission may authorize its officials to examine books and business records, take copies, ask for on the spot explanations and enter premises, but there is no obligation to comply. If a request made under article 14(1) does not prove to be sufficient, it can proceed under article 14(3) by making a decision ordering an undertaking to submit to investigation; this time the undertaking is bound to comply. There is, however, no necessity for the Commission to go through the preliminary stage of the procedure under 14(1). It can proceed directly to a decision under 14(3) without warning the company, and arrive unannounced.

Compliance is enforced with assistance of the 'competent authority' in the Member State. In the United Kingdom the competent authority is either the Secretary of State for Trade or the Director General for Fair Trading who can apply for appropriate injunctions to enforce the powers of the Commission. What happens in practice is that the Commission officials come armed with the decision ordering the company to submit to the investigation. If it refuses, an application is made *ex parte* in the Commercial Court for an injunction, like an *Anton Piller* order, restraining the company from destroying any documents and requiring it to admit the officials of the Commission to carry out their investigation.

It is difficult to know what advice to give to a client who is faced with a request for information from the Commission. The first point to note is that there is no right of silence. There may be a temptation to give inadequate information on the first request; but, carelessness at this stage may be difficult to rectify later on, since the Commission may be disinclined to believe a later explanation. Any statement which departs significantly from reality will amount to incorrect information within article 15, and will incur liability to a fine. If the initial request for information under article 11(1) is widely drawn, as is often the case, it may be best to wait for the Commission to demand information under article 11(5), since it must then specify what information is required.

If the inspector arrives uninvited there will be an explanatory memorandum attached to his warrant, setting out his powers. Article 14 does not specifically say that he has the power to search, but there is a duty to assist him to the extent of actually producing the specific documents required: Commission Decision 80/334 *Fabbrica Pisana* (OJ L75 21.3.80 p30). Tactically it is best to answer his questions fully, and favourable points should be emphasized rather than left for the hearing.

Legal professional privilege may be claimed, but only to a limited extent. Case 155/79 *A M & S Ltd* v. *EC Commission* [1982] ECR 1575, [1982] 2 CMLR 264 sets out the limits of legal privilege as it applies in Community law. Privilege may not be claimed in respect of communications to in-house lawyers. Communications to independent lawyers may be privileged if made after proceedings were commenced.

As has already been mentioned, a finding that an undertaking has infringed articles 85(1) or article 86 of the Treaty will result in a fine of up to 10 per cent of turnover. If an agreement is notified to the Commission, however, no fine can be imposed for acts done after notification and before the Commission decision provided that they fall within the limits of the activity described in the notification. Fines are enforced by registration in the High Court which then enforces them as if they were an ordinary judgment: RSC O.71.

Since the *Camera Case*, Case 792/79R *Camera Care Ltd* v. *EC Commission* [1980] ECR 131, [1980] 1 CMLR 334, it has been recognized that the Commission also has the power to make interim orders. An example of this is provided by the Commission Decision in *Brass Band Instruments* (OJ L286 9.10.87 p.36). This case has already been mentioned as a general illustration of the powers of the Commission (see Chapter 2). Boosey and Hawkes, the brass band instrument makers, had managed to obtain a dominant position in the market for brass band instruments. They refused to supply parts to their competitor, Brass Band Instruments. The Commission, on a complaint, by way of an interim decision, ordered Boosey and Hawkes to supply the parts on pain of a penalty of 1000 ECUs per day.

Co-operation with national courts

In *Garden Cottage Foods* v. *Milk Marketing Board* [1984] 1 AC 130, [1983] 3 CMLR 43 it was said that an abuse of a dominant position would give rise to an action in damages; articles 85 and 86 of the Treaty are directly applicable law. One can see, therefore, that in the Brass Bands Instruments case it would have been possible to apply for an interim injunction and damages rather than proceeding by way of a complaint to the Commission. The enforcement of EC competition law is thus a task that can be undertaken by either the Commission or the courts in Member States, but the Commission, because of its limited resources, prefers people to use their national courts.

In Case T–24/90 *Automec Srl* v. *EC Commission* [1992] 5 CMLR 431 the applicant was an Italian car dealer who complained that BMW had violated article 85 by refusing to continue his dealership. He asked the Commission to grant him an injunction to compel BMW to resume supplies. The Commission rejected his complaint because the Italian courts were already seized of the matter. He appealed to the Court of First Instance, who said that under article 85(1) the Commission was not empowered to grant an injunction ordering BMW to supply him. The Commission had a discretionary power to conduct an investigation, were entitled to prioritize matters in that regard, and were entitled to refer him to the Italian courts.

It was the *Automec* case that prompted the Commission to issue a Notice on Co-operation between National Courts and the Commission in Applying Articles 85 and 86 (OJ C39 13.2.93 p.6). The problem was, how to avoid conflicts and divide responsibility for the application of competition law between national courts and the Commission; the purpose of the notice was to achieve effective co-operation between them. In the notice the Commission points out the advantages of using national courts, namely that the Commission cannot award damages, that national courts can adopt interim measures more rapidly, that national courts can combine EC and national law claims, and that the Commission cannot award costs. The Commission, for its part, intends in future to devote itself to proceedings which have particular political, economic or legal significance to the Community; in ordinary cases notifications will be dealt with by a comfort letter, and complaints will be handled by national courts or authorities.

The notice, which does not relate to competition rules governing transport, suggests that national courts, before exercising their powers, should ascertain whether the conduct complained of has already been the subject of a decision, opinion or other official statement, such as a comfort letter, and take account of the Commission's powers. If the Commission has initiated a procedure, the courts should stay the matter before them.

The only exception to these principles is that 'old agreements', meaning agreements which, like the Net Book Agreement, were in force before Regulation 17 came into existence or before a Member State joined the Community, remain valid until the Commission has made its decision; this is explained in Case 48/72 *Brasserie de Haecht SA* v. *Wilkin-Janssen* [1973] ECR 77, [1973] CMLR 287. New agreements, although notified to the Commission, do not gain any interim validity and are therefore vulnerable to civil action.

It is anticipated that national courts will find sufficient guidance to assist them in the application of EC competition law from the case law of the European Court, the block exemption regulations, and the various notices issued by the Commission, but if that is not enough they may, within the limits of their national procedural law, ask the Commission for assistance. The Commission can provide the court with procedural information, such as whether the Commission has officially initiated a procedure, can be consulted on points of law, can be asked to give an interim opinion on whether an agreement is eligible for individual exemption, and will provide statistical and other similar information. The courts of the United Kingdom have yet to determine how this role will be fitted, if at all, to their procedure; though the notice speaks of the Commission as a neutral and objective *amicus curiae*, one wonders if it might not appear merely impertinent.

State aids

This chapter has been concerned with the law of competition as it applies to private undertakings. Distortion of competition can also arise as a result of direct state intervention by way of aid to industry. Each year the Commission publishes an Annual Report on Competition Policy; more than half the contents are devoted to state aids. Article 92(1) of the EC Treaty reads as follows:

> Save as otherwise provided in this Treaty, any aid granted by a Member State or through State resources in any form whatsoever which distorts or threatens to distort competition by favouring certain undertakings or the production of certain goods shall, in so far as it affects trade between Member States, be incompatible with the Common Market.

No definition of aid is given in the Treaty but it certainly includes subsidies: Case 30/59 *Steenkolenmijnen* v. *High Authority* [1961] ECR 1. It also includes tax exemptions, preferential interest rates, guarantees of loans on particularly favourable terms and other similar gratuitous advantages granted through state resources. And, in Case 310/85 *Deufil GmbH & Co* v. *EC Commission* [1987] ECR 901, 1988 3 CMLR 687, in which the applicant claimed that sums paid to a German textile factory were not aid because they were, consistent with article 130 of the Treaty, calculated to improve general economic development, the Court said that state aid is defined not by its causes but by its effects.

In Case 730/79 *Philip Morris Holland BV* v. *EC Commission* [1980] ECR 2671, [1981] 2 CMLR 321 a question of whether aid affected trade between Member States arose with regard to aid which the Dutch Government proposed to provide towards the enlargement of a cigarette factory. The Court said that, when financial aid strengthens the position of an undertaking compared with other undertakings competing in intra-Community trade, the latter must be regarded as affected by that aid. The aid in question was destined for a company organized for international trade, a high proportion of whose production was destined for export to other Member States.

Not all aid is incompatible with the common market. Article 92(2) contains exceptions in the case of aid having a social character, or designed to make good natural disasters, or made to certain areas of Germany to compensate for the economic disadvantage caused by the former division of that country. Aid may be permitted to promote the economic development of areas where the standard of living is low and for certain other purposes and, since Maastricht, to promote culture and heritage conservation where it does not affect trading conditions and competition to an extent that is contrary to the common interest.

Under article 93 of the Treaty the Commission has the duty to keep under review systems of aid in Member States. If, after giving notice to the parties concerned to submit their comments, the Commission finds that aid granted by a Member State is incompatible with the common market or is being misused, it has to decide that the State concerned shall abolish or alter the aid within a time limit fixed by the Commission. If the Member State does not comply the Commission, or any interested State, can refer the matter directly to the Court of Justice.

In Case 6/64 *Costa* v. *ENEL* [1964] ECR 585, [1964] CMLR 425 the question whether articles 92 to 94 of the Treaty were of direct effect was discussed. It was held that none of those articles is of direct effect, except for the final provision of article 93(3). This is a procedural provision; a Member State may not put its proposed aid into operation until the procedure in paragraph 2 of the article has resulted in a final decision. There is, thus, the possibility of challenging in a national court the grant of state aid where article 93(3) is not complied with.

Chapter 13

Company Law

There would be no point in creating a common market if a company operating in the Community was unable to choose where to establish itself, or if a company established in one Member State was not permitted to provide services in another. The right to free movement and freedom of establishment are established by the EC Treaty but, nevertheless, wide variations in the company law of Member States still create obstacles to free movement. The *Daily Mail* case, discussed below, is a case which demonstrates the difficulties which can arise when companies choose to move from one Member State to another.

Community legislation in the area of company law is concerned with harmonization of the laws of Member States. Harmonization is based on article 54(3)(g) of the EC Treaty, which speaks of 'coordinating to the necessary extent the safeguards which ... are required by Member States of companies or firms ... with a view to making such safeguards equivalent throughout the Community'. Article 58 of the Treaty states that companies or firms are to be treated, for the purposes of the chapter on the right of establishment, in the same way as natural persons who are nationals of Member States; 'companies or firms' includes cooperative societies, and other legal persons governed by public or private law, save for those which are non-profit making.

Article 100 of the Treaty would appear to be a more appropriate vehicle for the activities of the Commission because it deals with approximation of laws. The difficulty was that, until amendments were inserted by the Single European Act, article 100 always required the unanimity of the Council.

Under article 220 of the Treaty Member States can make conventions for 'the mutual recognition of companies or firms ... the retention of legal personality in the event of transfer from one country to another, and the possibility of mergers between companies or firms governed by the laws of different countries'. There is a Convention on the Mutual Recognition of Companies which was entered into in 1968. No doubt it would be of interest if it was ever ratified, but since this requires unanimity it will probably never happen.

The Harmonization Directives

Nine directives on the harmonization of company law have so far been implemented. Others are languishing as mere proposals; the so-called 'Vredeling Directive' is the most famous of these. It suggests that large companies with a complex structure should regularly provide information to their employees on production plans, management changes, and other matters which might concern them. A convenient collection of proposals, directives, and other documents relating to company law is published by the Commission and obtainable from HMSO: *Harmonization of Company Law in the European Community*, ISBN 92–825–9578–1.

The importance of the directives in interpreting the corresponding British legislation is not to be underestimated. The purpose of these directives is to alter the relevant legal provisions of each Member State so as to achieve the same result; there ought not, therefore, to be any development of diverging interpretations in different jurisdictions. The European Court has said in Case 14/83 *von Colson* v. *Land Nordrhein-Westfalen* [1984] ECR 1891, [1986] 2 CMLR 430 that, in applying law which implements a directive, national courts are required to interpret national law in the light of the wording and purpose of the directive. In *Litster* v. *Forth Dry Dock & Engineering Co Ltd* [1989] 2 WLR 634, [1989] 1 All ER 1134 Lord Templeman said that: 'The courts of the United Kingdom are under a duty to follow the practice of the European Court by giving a purposive construction to directives and to regulations issued for the purpose of complying with directives'. It follows from those cases that it is not safe to interpret company legislation without reference to the European legislation. The main directives on harmonization are as follows.

First Council Directive of 9th March 1968 (EEC) 68/151 (OJ L65 14.3.68 p8)

This directive protects third parties dealing with companies by stipulating that basic company documents should be disclosed, restricting the grounds upon which obligations entered into by the company can be held to be invalid, and limiting the circumstances in which nullity can be ordered. In the case of contracts made before a company has acquired legal personality the persons who acted in its name are liable. It was one of the first provisions of Community law to be incorporated into an English statute; it was adopted by means of section 9 of the European Communities Act 1972. Implementing legislation is now to be found in Sections 18, 35–35A, 36, 42, 351, 711 and Schedule 22 of the Companies Act 1985.

The directive has been adopted in all the Member States and it was utilized by the defendant in Case C–106/89 *Marleasing SA* v. *La Comercial* [1990] ECR 4135, [1992] 1 CMLR 305, which established that a court must interpret its national law in the light of the wording and purpose of the directive, in order to prevent a declaration of nullity of a public company on any grounds other than those set out in article 11 of the directive. For the facts of this case see Chapter 3.

Second Council Directive of 13th December 1976 (EEC) 77/91 (OJ L26 31.1.77 p1)

This directive safeguards shareholders and creditors of public limited companies in respect of their formation and the main-tenance of capital. It supplements the First Directive and was orig-inally implemented by the Companies Act 1980, but is now reflected in Parts IV,V and VIII of the Companies Act 1985.

Third Council Directive of 9th October 1978 (EEC) 78/855 (OJ L295 20.10.78 p36)

The Third Directive is concerned with the regulation of mergers. It is complemented by the Sixth Directive. Implementing legislation is to be found in the Companies (Mergers and Divisions) Regu-lations 1987, SI 1987 No 1991, and the Insurance Companies (Mergers and Divisions) Regulations 1987, SI 1987 No 2118.

Fourth Council Directive of 25th July 1978 (EEC) 78/660 (OJ L222 14.8.78 p11)

This directive, which was amended by Council Directive (EEC) 84/569 (OJ L314 4.12.84 p28), concerns the layout of accounts and

the basis on which they are prepared. It was first implemented by
the Companies Act 1981 which in turn was consolidated in Part VII
of the Companies Act 1985. Implementing legislation includes the
Companies (Modified Accounts) (Amendment) Regulations 1986,
SI 1986/1865, and the Companies Act 1985 (Accounts of Small and
Medium Sized Enterprises and Publication of Accounts in ECUs)
Regulations 1992, SI 1992/2452.

Sixth Council Directive of 17th December 1982 (EEC) 82/891 (OJ L378 31.12.82 p47)

This directive complements the Third Directive and concerns the
division of companies where assets are acquired by other
companies. The implementing legislation is to be found in the
statutory instruments which implement the Third Directive
(above).

Seventh Council Directive of 13th June 1983 (EEC) 83/394 (OJ L193 18.7.83 p1)

This concerns the preparation of consolidated accounts by parent
companies. It was implemented by the Companies Act 1989, Part I.

Eighth Council Directive of 10th April 1984 (EEC) 84/253 (OJ L126 12.5.84 p20)

This makes provisions for the qualifications of auditors. It was
implemented by the Companies Act 1989, Part II, the Company
Auditors (Examinations) Regulations 1990, SI 1990 No 1146, and
the Companies Act 1989 (Register of Auditors and Information
about Audit Firms) Regulations 1991, SI 1991 No 1566.

Eleventh Council Directive of 30 December 1989 (EEC) 89/666 (OJ L395 30.12.89 p36)

This makes disclosure requirements in respect of branches established in Member States by certain foreign companies, including
companies not governed by the laws of Member States. Its purpose
is to protect persons dealing with foreign companies that carry on

business in a Member State. It is implemented by the Companies Act 1985 (Disclosure of Branches and Bank Accounts) Regulations 1992, SI 1992/3178, and the Overseas Companies and Credit and Financial Institutions (Branch Disclosure) Regulations 1992, SI 1992/3179.

Twelfth Council Directive of 21 December 1989 (EEC) 89/667 (OJ L395 30.12.89 p40)

Some Member States, namely Germany, Denmark, France, Belgium and the Netherlands, permit the formation of single–member private limited liability companies. The Twelfth Directive is designed to harmonize laws relating to this kind of company.

Proposals

There are gaps in the above list. The proposed Fifth Directive (OJ C240 9.9.83 p2) is still a proposal because of the political difficulty that it provides for employee participation in the management of a company. It overlaps with the Draft Vredeling Directive (OJ C217 12.8.83 p3) procedures for informing and consulting the employees of companies with complex structures. No one expects these proposals to be adopted.

But, in the near future, it is likely that further proposals for harmonization of company law will be introduced. An informal draft of a Ninth Directive on group liability has been circulated, and there is a proposal for a Tenth Directive on cross border mergers (OJ C23 25.1.85 p11). There is a proposal for a Thirteenth Directive on takeovers and other general bids (OJ C240 26.9.90 p7).

Moving home – the Daily Mail *case*

In Case 81/87 *R* v. *HM Treasury ex p Daily Mail* [1989] 2 WLR 908, [1989] 1 All ER 328 an attempt was made to take advantage of articles 52 and 58 of the Treaty. Article 52 confers a right to freedom of establishment and article 58 states that companies are to be treated in the same way as natural persons. The applicant, an investment holding company, was resident for tax purposes in the United Kingdom. It discovered that there were certain tax advantages in moving to the Netherlands, whose legislation does not prevent foreign companies from setting up their central management there. The only fly in the ointment is that a company cannot transfer its residence for tax purposes without the consent of the Treasury. After a period of fruitless bargaining with the Treasury the matter came before the European Court on an article 177 reference.

The Court held that the Treaty cannot be interpreted as conferring on Companies a right to transfer to another Member State while retaining their status as companies incorporated under the legislation of the original Member State. The case shows how far real free movement in the Community is dependent upon harmonization of tax laws.

But, in *R* v. *Inland Revenue Commissioners ex parte Commerzbank AG* [1993] 4 All E R 37, the European Court held that a German bank with a branch in the United Kingdom had suffered from discrimination. The bank claimed a repayment supplement, a sum equivalent to lost interest, on a tax refund; but only a company resident in the United Kingdom was entitled, under English law, to recoup this money. However, the European Court held that this unequal treatment amounted to discrimination contrary to articles 52 and 58 of the Treaty. It follows that sometimes it is possible to gain a tax advantage by relying on article 52.

European Economic Interest Groupings

The Commission has been anxious to encourage cooperative enterprises between European companies. Council Regulation 2137/85 (OJ L199 31.7.85 p1) has introduced a new vehicle for use by companies wishing to set up joint ventures. These entities, known as European Economic Interest Groupings (EEIG), are not subject to the regulations imposed by national company laws. The relevant United Kingdom legislation is in the European Economic Interest Grouping Regulations 1989, SI 1989 No 638.

The purpose of an Economic Interest Grouping is not to make profits for itself, but to facilitate or develop the economic activities of its members. It cannot exercise management powers over its own members or any other undertaking. It cannot hold the shares of its members. It cannot make loans to directors of companies where that is restricted by the law of a Member State. It can, however, hold the shares of non-member companies.

The contract by which a European Interest Grouping is founded must include the name and address of the interest grouping, its objects and the names and addresses of its members. From the date of its registration in Britain a European Interest Grouping becomes a body corporate under the name in the contract of foundation. The Insolvency Act 1986 has been modified to allow for the winding up of a grouping as if it were an unregistered company under Part V of the Act.

Societas Europea

The Commission has long advocated the idea of a new kind of company formed on Community lines; from time to time different versions of draft proposals for a regulation creating a European company are circulated or published in the *Official Journal*. It is one of the measures which was listed in the Commission White Paper on completing the internal market and was first presented as a proposal in 1970 but progress has been slow. The latest version, a proposal for a Council Regulation on the Statute for a European Company (OJ C176 8.7.91 p1) will, if adopted, enable the formation of a European public limited company. Such a *Societas Europea*, or SE, will have a minimum capital of 100 000 ECUs. Eventually an entirely new area of directly applicable Company law may develop.

Chapter 14

Social Policy

The EC Treaty has a profound effect on social policy. The case law in this area has been concerned with the interpretation of the equal treatment provisions of the Treaty, the extent to which those provisions are of direct effect, and conflict with national legislation.

Articles 117 to 122 of the Treaty contain the basic social provisions; these articles are frequently referred to as the Social Chapter and they have been left almost unaltered by Maastricht. Articles 123 to 125 provide for the setting up of a European Social Fund which finances vocational training and other schemes to improve employment opportunities. Articles 126 and 127 comprise a separate chapter devoted to education, vocational training, and youth.

Under article 117 of the Treaty Member States have agreed upon the need to promote improved working conditions and an improved standard of living for workers. This is seen as a development which will arise not only from the functioning of the common market, which will favour the harmonization of social systems, but also from the procedures provided for in the Treaty, and from the approximation of provisions laid down by law, regulation, or administrative action.

Article 118a was inserted by the Single European Act. It provides for Member States to pay particular attention to encouraging improvements, especially in the working environment, as regards the health and safety of workers.

Article 119 provides for equal pay without discrimination based on sex. It has affected the law of the United Kingdom to a marked extent and the full text is as follows:

Article 119. Each Member State shall during the first stage ensure and subsequently maintain the application of the principle that men and women should receive equal pay for equal work.

For the purpose of this Article, 'pay' means the ordinary basic or minimum wage or salary and any other consideration, whether in cash or kind, which the worker receives, directly or indirectly, in respect of his employment from his employer.

Equal pay without discrimination based on sex means:

(a) that pay for the same work at piece rates shall be calculated on the basis of the same unit of measurement;
(b) that pay for work at time rates shall be the same for the same job.

The Social Charter

The Community Charter of the Fundamental Social Rights of Workers is simply a solemn declaration that was adopted by the Council in December 1989. It has no legal force, but is supposed to demonstrate the identity of Europe in the social field, and lists a series of rights for workers. The list includes the following: a statement on the right to freedom of movement; protection with regard to living and working conditions; the right to adequate social benefits; the right to freedom of association and collective bargaining; the right to vocational training; the right to equal treatment; the right of workers to be consulted and to participate in management decisions; the right to health and safety at work; and, the right to protection of children, the elderly and the disabled. The right to strike is qualified in that it is made subject to national regulations and collective agreements.

During the Maastricht negotiations the United Kingdom opposed the widening of the social scope of the EC Treaty. The other eleven Member States proposed to implement the Social Charter by making changes to the social chapter of the EC Treaty, but the text of the social chapter was not altered, because the United Kingdom refused to agree to their proposals. Therefore the eleven made an agreement to implement the Social Charter between themselves. A Protocol on Social Policy, annexed to the Maastricht Treaty, authorizes the eleven to take amongst themselves, and apply so far as they are concerned, the acts and decisions necessary to give effect to their agreement; the text of the agreement is set out after the Protocol and states, *inter alia*, that the eleven shall have as their objectives the promotion of employment, improved living and working conditions, proper social protection, and dialogue between management and labour. The United Kingdom cannot take part in the deliberations and the adoption by the Council of Commission proposals made on the basis of the

Protocol; this is unfortunate because, in the area of social policy, EC law will not develop homogeneously.

The Defrenne *cases*

The development of the law of equal treatment owes much to Miss Defrenne, an air hostess, whose conditions of service with Sabena Airlines required her to retire at the fatal age of forty. This requirement did not apply to her male colleagues. In proceedings before the Belgian *Conseil d'Etat* she complained that a decree concerning the pensions payable to air crew, which was issued within the framework of the general state scheme for retirement pensions, was contrary to article 119.

The European Court ruled that a retirement pension which is established within the framework of a social security scheme laid down by legislation does not constitute consideration which the worker receives indirectly in respect of his or her employment within the meaning of the second paragraph of article 119: Case 80/70 *Gabrielle Defrenne* v. *Belgian State* [1971] ECR 445, [1974] 1 CMLR 494.

Miss Defrenne also brought a second action, this time before the *Tribunal de travail*. In this, Case 43/75 *Gabrielle Defrenne* v. *Société Anonyme Belge de Navigation Aérienne Sabena* [1976] ECR 455, [1976] 2 CMLR 98, she was more successful. Miss Defrenne claimed that the salary paid to her had been less than that to which a male steward would have been entitled. Two questions were referred to the European Court: (a) whether article 119 was directly applicable; and (b) whether article 119 had become applicable in the internal law of the Member States by virtue of measures adopted by the authorities of the Community, or whether the national legislature alone was to be regarded as competent in the matter.

In answer to the first question the Court replied that, where the discrimination was direct, article 119 can be relied on before national courts. A distinction was drawn between, first, direct and overt discrimination which may be identified solely with the aid of the criteria based on equal work and equal pay referred to by the article and, second, indirect and disguised discrimination which can only be identified by reference to more explicit implementing provisions of Community or national character. This direct discrimination can be detected 'on the basis of a purely legal analysis of the situation'. It follows that where one can show direct discrimination article 119 can be relied on, both against the State and against private individuals.

The terminology used to describe those circumstances when article 119 has direct effect is confusing. Advocate General Warner in Case 96/80 *Jenkins* v. *Kingsgate* [1981] ECR 911, [1981] 2 CMLR 24 explains it more clearly: 'Article 119 is, in my opinion, more accurately described as not having direct effect where a court cannot apply its provisions by reference to the simple criteria that those provisions themselves lay down and where, consequently, implementing legislation, either Community or national, is necessary to lay down the relevant criteria.'

The second question, which asked the Court to say who was competent to make measures to implement article 119, was answered in the following way. Although the article was addressed to the Member States, in that it imposed on them a duty to apply the principle of equal pay, that duty did not exclude the competence of the Community. Even in areas where article 119 has no direct effect the national legislature does not have exclusive power to implement the article; implementation may be by a combination of Community and national measures.

Having established that article 119 had direct effect the Court then had to deal with the practical effect of such a judgment; many thousands of women would be filing claims for arrears of pay. The damages would, indeed, be enormous. Fortunately the Court was able to call upon the principle of legal certainty and ruled that the effect of its decision, save for Miss Defrenne herself, was not retrospective.

The equality directives

Council Directive (EEC) 75/117 (OJ L45 19.2.75 p19) is designed to encourage Member States to apply article 119. They are required to abolish laws which are contrary to the principle of equal pay, and ensure that wage agreements and contracts containing discriminatory conditions are rendered void. In the *Sabena* case (above) it was said that Directive 75/117 does not derogate in any way from article 119. In litigation between private individuals it will not be possible to rely on it directly. It serves, however, to explain article 119 of the Treaty; the principle of equal pay is defined in the directive as meaning: '... for the same work or for work to which equal value is attributed, the elimination of all discrimination on grounds of sex with regard to all aspects and conditions of remuneration'.

Council Directive (EEC) 76/207 (OJ L39 14.2.76 p40) is the directive which puts into effect the principle of equal treatment with regard to access to employment, vocational training and promotion, and working conditions. Other directives deal with the following: equal treatment in social security, Council Directive (EEC) 79/7 (OJ L6 10.1.79 p24); equal treatment in occupational social security schemes, Council Directive (EEC) 86/378 (OJ L225 12.8.86 p40); and, equal treatment in self employment, Council Directive (EEC) 86/613 (OJ L359 19.12.86 p56).

Transfers, insolvency and redundancy

Apart from the equal treatment directives there are other directives which give protection for workers in the case of collective redundancies, transfers of undertakings, and the employer's insolvency. Council Directive (EEC) 75/129 (OJ L48 22.2.75 p29) on collective redundancies provides for the implementation of procedures for consultation and notification. Council Directive (EEC) 80/987 (OJ L283 28.10.80 p23) gives protection to workers on insolvency by requiring Member States to take measures to ensure that guarantee institutions guarantee the payment of workers' outstanding claims.

Council Directive (EEC) 77/187 (OJ L61 5.3.77 p26) requires Member States to make legislation making the transferee of an undertaking liable for existing contracts of employment. In the United Kingdom the implementing legislation is the Transfer of Undertakings (Protection of Employment) Regulations SI 1981 No 1794, which, as originally drafted, defined undertakings as 'commercial ventures'. Workers affected by privatization schemes complained that the domestic law did not implement the directive, because the directive contains no such definition. The European Court has not yet attempted a definition, but the dustmen of Eastbourne Borough Council, who were the appellants in *Wren* v. *Eastbourne Borough Council* (*The Times* 18 August 1993), and who found themselves out of work when their Council contracted out their work to a private employer, persuaded the Employment Appeal Tribunal that the phrase 'in the nature of a commercial venture' which appears in the implementing regulation was to be construed in accordance with the law of the United Kingdom but not in a way which conflicted with the guidance given by the European Court. Guidance can be found in Case 24/85 *Spijkers* v.

Benedik [1986] ECR 1119, in which the European Court said that the question for the Industrial Tribunal in such a case was whether, in all the circumstances, the business had been transferred as a going concern, and in Case C–29/91 *Dr Sophie Redmond Stichting* v. *Bartol and others* [1992] ECR I–3189 in which the Advocate General indicated that the word 'undertaking' should be given a wide meaning and was not necessarily confined to commercial concerns.

After the dustmen won their case, the Transfer of Undertakings (Protection of Employment) Regulations were amended, by section 33 of the Trade Union Reform and Employment Rights Act 1993, in order to confirm that employees in non-commercial ventures are protected. But the amendments are not retrospective, nor do they meet all the requirements in the directive for consultation and provision of information to representatives of workers. Concerned that further litigation would damage its plans for privatisation the United Kingdom, in December 1993, at a meeting of the European Council, persuaded the Community to redraft the directive; in 1994 it will be changed.

Infringement proceedings

Infringement proceedings have been brought by the Commission against the United Kingdom. For example, in Case 61/81 *EC Commission* v. *United Kingdom* [1982] ECR 2601, [1982] 3 CMLR 284 the complaint was that there was a failure to comply with Directive 75/117 because there was a lacuna in the Equal Pay Act 1970: workers could not have their work rated as of equal value with comparable work if the employer had no system of job classification. As a result of these proceedings amendments, including a new section 2A, were added to the Act. In Case 165/82 *EC Commission* v. *United Kingdom* [1983] ECR 3431, [1984] 1 CMLR 44 the proceedings concerned a failure to implement Directive 76/207 because of the exclusion of private households and employers with less than five employees from the employment provisions of the Sex Discrimination Act 1975. Section 1 of the Sex Discrimination Act 1986 subsequently narrowed this exemption; the Act is a collection of provisions designed to bring British law into line with Community law.

Interpretation of article 119

The Defrenne cases serve to show that 'pay' does not include state pension benefits, and that article 119 will be of direct effect in those cases where discrimination is direct. Directive 75/117 explains that the 'principle of equal pay' means the elimination of discrimination for the same work, or for work to which equal value is attributed.

Whether job classification can take account of muscular effort was discussed in Case 237/85 *Rummler* v. *Dato-Druck* [1987] 3 CMLR 127, [1987] ICR 774. A dispute had arisen in a German printing firm where there was a grading system according to the physical effort involved in the work. The European Court ruled that a job classification system is not discriminatory merely because one of its criteria is based on characteristics more commonly found in men.

The problem of indirect discrimination was discussed in Case 170/84 *Bilka-Kaufhaus GmbH* v. *Weber von Hartz* [1986] ECR 1607, [1986] 2 CMLR 701. Mrs Weber complained that, in the department store owned by Bilka-Kaufhaus, only full-time employees were entitled to a pension. This was unfair to women employees who, for the most part, worked part-time. The European Court, in considering whether this practice was contrary to article 119, followed its judgment in Case 96/80 *Jenkins* v. *Kingsgate (Clothing Productions) Ltd* [1981] ECR 911,[1981] 2 CMLR 24. In that judgment the Court had considered the question whether the payment of a lower hourly rate for part-time work than for full-time work was compatible with article 119. The Court used a concept of objective justification which is applied in the following way: if a much lower proportion of women than of men work full-time, the exclusion of part-time workers from, for example, an occupational pension scheme is contrary to article 119 where, taking into account the difficulties encountered by women workers in working full time, it cannot be explained by factors which exclude any discrimination on grounds of sex. The test of 'objective justification' involves the application of the principle of proportionality. In other words, does the means chosen for achieving the pay policy correspond to a real need on the part of the undertaking, and is it appropriate with a view to achieving the objective in question, and necessary to that end?

Conflict with national legislation

A problem which arises whenever Community law impinges on British legislation is the question of what is to happen when there is a conflict. This problem has been particularly pertinent in employment law because of the tendency for British legislation to lag behind Europe. The view of the European Court was expressed in Case 106/77 *Amministrazione delle Finanze dello Stato* v. *Simmenthal SpA* [1978] ECR 629, [1978] CMLR 263, in which the Court ruled that Community law has priority even over the constitutional laws of a Member State. In Case 14/83 *Von Colson* v. *Land Nordrhein-Westfalen* [1984] ECR 1891, [1986] 2 CMLR 430 the European Court was asked to consider a question which arose when Werl prison refused to engage two social workers for reasons relating to their sex. They claimed damages under the German equal treatment laws. The difficulty was that, although the national law was supposed to transpose Council Directive 76/207 into German law, it did not do so in a way which provided for adequate damages. In its judgment the Court said that in applying the national law, and in particular the provisions of a national law specifically introduced in order to implement Directive 76/207, national courts are required to interpret national law in the light of the wording and purpose of the directive. In the operative part of the judgment this sentiment was expressed slightly differently: 'It is for the national court to interpret and apply the legislation adopted for the implementation of the directive in conformity with the requirements of Community law, in so far as it is given discretion to do so under national law'.

In Case C–106/89 *Marleasing SA* v. *La Comercial Internacional de Alimentacion SA* [1992] 1 CMLR 305, where the question was whether the First Company Law Directive, Council Directive (EEC) 68/151 (OJ L65 14.3.68 p8), had been implemented in Spanish law, the Court said that it was for the Spanish court so to interpret its law, in the light of the wording and purpose of the directive, as to preclude a declaration of nullity of a company on a ground other than those listed in article 11 of the directive; the Court now had confidence not to say that this duty should be limited to the discretion conferred by national law. For the facts of this case the reader should turn to Chapter 3 of this book, where it is considered in connection with the doctrine of useful effect.

It is against the background of the decisions in *Simmenthal*, *Marleasing* and *Von Colson* that one has to consider the English cases. In Case 152/84 *Marshall* v. *Southampton and South West Hampshire Area Health Authority* [1986] ECR 723, [1986] 1 CMLR 688 Miss Marshall was able to circumvent the problem of what to do when Community law is not sufficiently implemented by a British statute by relying on the doctrine of direct effect. Her complaint was that she had suffered unlawful discrimination contrary to both the Sex Discrimination Act 1975 and Council Directive 76/207, the equal treatment directive. She had been required to retire at 60 instead of 65.

In the Industrial Tribunal her claim under the Sex Discrimination Act was dismissed because the act permitted discrimination on the ground of sex where it arose out of a 'provisions in relation to retirement'.

The Industrial Tribunal, however, upheld her claim in so far as it was based on the directive. The Health Authority appealed. Two questions were referred to the European Court: (a) whether dismissing her solely because she had passed her sixtieth birthday, pursuant to the policy followed by the respondent, was an act of discrimination prohibited by the directive, and (b) whether, if the answer to that question was in the affirmative, the directive could be relied on notwithstanding that it was inconsistent with the Sex Discrimination Act.

The European Court held that there was discrimination and, furthermore, that she could rely on the directive as against the Health Authority, and set it up against the inconsistent section of the Sex Discrimination Act. It was argued by the appellants that a directive could never impose obligations directly on individuals, and that it could have effect against a Member State only when the state was acting as a public authority, and not when it was acting as an employer. The Court met this by saying that it did not matter if the Health Authority was only acting as an employer; the Authority was an emanation of the state, and liable in whatever capacity it acted.

In *McCarthy's Ltd* v. *Smith* [1979] 3 CMLR 44 & 381, [1978] 1 WLR 849 the Court of Appeal had to consider whether a woman was entitled to claim equal pay in comparison with a man. The man was not employed contemporaneously, having left some months before Mrs Smith joined the company. In 1975 a section had been inserted into the Equal Pay Act 1970 which introduced an 'equality clause' into a woman's contract; it was drafted in such a way that it applied only if the woman was employed contemporaneously with the man. Clearly this conflicted with article 119 of the Treaty. Lord Denning in a dissenting judgment said that: 'In construing our statute we are entitled to look to the Treaty as an aid to its construction; but not only as an aid but as an overriding force. If on close investigation it should appear that our legislation is deficient or inconsistent with Community law by some oversight of our draftsmen then it is our bounden duty to give priority to Community law'.

The Courts have had some reluctance to see Lord Denning's point of view. In *Garland* v. *British Rail Engineering Ltd* [1982] 2 CMLR 174, [1983] AC 751 Lord Diplock said that, with regard to Community measures, the words of a statute were 'to be construed, if they are reasonably capable of bearing such a meaning, as intended to carry out the obligation and not to be inconsistent with it'. In *Duke* v. *GEC Reliance Ltd* [1988] AC 618, [1988] 2 WLR 359 Mrs Duke tried to take advantage of Directive 76/207 in order to claim damages because she was obliged to retire at 60. Her employer was not an 'emanation of the state' so she could not take advantage of the direct effect of the directive as Miss Marshall had done in her action against the Health Authority. Lord Templeman said that, despite the *Von Colson* case, it would be unfair to the respondent to distort the construction of the Sex Discrimination Act 1975 in order to accommodate the equal treatment directive; his reasoning took advantage of the now discredited final words of the operative part of the judgment in *Von Colson*, which said that the duty of the national court extended only so far as it was given discretion under national law.

The House of Lords now takes a more radical course. In *Pickstone* v. *Freemans plc* [1989] AC 66, [1988] 3 WLR 265 five women warehouse operatives claimed that their work was of equal value to that of a male warehouse checker. As we have seen, in Case 61/81 *EC Commission* v. *United Kingdom* [1982] ECR 2601, [1982] 3 CMLR 284 the European Court ruled that there had been a failure to implement Directive 75/117 because there was no system for a woman to get her work rated as of equal value with comparable work. Accordingly, the Secretary of State for Employment made a regulation which introduced some amendments to the Equal Pay Act 1970. Alas, there was still a gap. On a strict reading of the amended section 1(2) of the Act it was possible to say that if one man was paid the same as the five women for the same work the comparison had to be made with him: not with all the other men doing work which was different but of equal value. The House of Lords grasped the nettle by simply applying a purposive approach to interpreting the Act; in other words, it was possible to fill in the gap.

The case was followed in *Litster* v. *Forth Dry Dock Co Ltd* [1989] 2 WLR 634, [1989] 1 All ER 1134 where a problem arose in relation to the Transfer of Undertakings (Protection of Employment) Regulations 1981, that were supposed to implement Directive 77/187 which provides protection for workers on the transfer of the undertaking. The employer argued that the plain meaning of the words in those regulations was that the employee had to be employed at the time of the transfer; by dismissing the employee, waiting a few hours, and then re-employing him it was possible to circumvent their effect. The House of Lords did not agree. Lord Templeman said that: 'The courts of the United Kingdom are under a duty to follow the practice of the European Court by giving a purposive construction to directives and to regulations issued for the purpose of complying with directives'.

It follows from the above that when confronted with legislation inspired by Community measures it is necessary to consider an entirely new way of interpreting the work of our draftsmen. If a statute is to be interpreted by Community canons of construction the rules are presumably not limited to the purposive approach: it may also be a contextual approach.

Since Cases C–6/90 and C–9/90 *Frankovich* v. *Republic of Italy* and *Bonifaci* v. *Republic of Italy* [1993] 2 CMLR 66, a further line of attack lies open to those who complain that they have not been accorded the benefit of an EC Directive, namely an action for damages against the state. See Chapter 7 of this book for an explanation of this case.

The Barber case

Case C–262/88 *Barber* v. *Guardian Royal Exchange Assurance Group* [1990] 2 All ER 660 shows the havoc wrought by the insistence of the European Court on the priority of European law, even, some might suggest, the priority of the jurisprudence of the Court over the intentions expressed in the directives of the Council. Mr Barber had a company pension, a contracted–out scheme entirely financed by his employer. At the age of 52 he was made redundant. When he got over the shock he discovered that a woman in his position was entitled to an immediate pension, but he was not. Under the terms of the scheme the normal retirement age for women was 57, and for men it was 62: but, in the case of a redundancy an immediate pension was payable for a woman at the age of 50, and for a man at 55. He went to the Employment Appeal Tribunal complaining of discrimination contrary to article 119 of the Treaty. His complaint about the breach of Directives 75/117 on equal treatment, and 76/207 on equal pay, could not succeed because they were not directly effective, nor could he rely upon the Sex Discrimination Act 1975, because that contained an exception in the case of arrangements relating to death or retirement. The Employment Appeal Tribunal said that he could not rely on article 119 either, because access to pensions benefits was a question of equal treatment and therefore nothing to do with article 119.

There was much to be said for this view, particularly when one comes to consider Council Directive 79/7 on the progressive implementation of the principle of equal treatment for men and women in matters of social security, which authorized Member States to defer compulsory implementation of the principle of equal treatment, with regard to the determination of pensionable age for the purpose of granting old age pensions. That exception was incorporated in Council Directive 86/378 on the implementation of the principle of equal treatment for men and women in occupational social security schemes. In the light of those provisions one might be forgiven for thinking that article 119 did not apply to contracted-out schemes.

But the European Court was not concerned with such commonsense. It ruled that money paid under a contracted out scheme was pay within article 119; it did, however, concede, in the same way as it did in the *Defrenne* case (above), that the effect of its judgment should not be retrospective, except in the case of Mr Barber himself. In case the Court had not made itself sufficiently clear, the second protocol to the Maastricht Treaty states that benefits under occupational social security schemes are not considered as pay within article 119, in so far as they are attributable to periods before 17 May 1990, the date of the judgment.

The future

The United Kingdom has not subscribed to the Social Charter. That does not mean that it will be any less bound by provisions properly based upon the Treaty. Proposals exist for directives requiring large undertakings with establishments in more than one Member State to have a European Works Council (OJ C39 15.2.91 p10), and for a directive on the organization of working time, including arrangements for night workers, annual paid holidays, rest periods and so on (OJ C124 15.5.91 p8), and for a directive dealing with workers temporarily posted to other Member States (OJ C225 30.8.91 p6). These proposals give some idea of the policies adopted by the Council in its third action programme on equal opportunities adopted in May 1991.

Chapter 15

The Environment

Strange contradictions lurk about in environmental law, as the following example will show.

Nitrate in ground water is associated with the large scale production of winter wheat. In autumn microbes are active in the soil, and they create nitrates that eventually pollute ground water. Winter wheat is produced in such quantity because of the generous intervention prices set under the Common Agricultural Policy. Therefore Community law affects the quality of our tap water.

In order to control the quality of drinking water, Council Directive (EEC) 80/778 states that the nitrate content of drinking water may not exceed 50 milligrams per litre. The Commission has brought an action against the United Kingdom, Case C–337/89 *Commission* v. *United Kingdom* (25 November 1992 *transcript*), for failure to implement this directive. The complaint was, *inter alia*, that in 28 supply zones in England and Wales the nitrate level exceeded the above limit. The United Kingdom argued that the directive ought to be read as imposing not a strict liability to keep below that limit, but a mere duty to take all practical steps to that end. But, the European Court held that practical difficulties were not an excuse, and the United Kingdom was convicted of failing to fulfil its obligations.

Here is a question that was not considered in that case: may there not be a lack of proportionality in a law which requires Member States to prevent what the European Community has created in the first place? The problem does not have a simple solution, because nitrates take years to soak down to ground water; today's legislation cannot eliminate the legacy of twenty years of high intervention prices for wheat.

The problem of nitrates in drinking water will help the reader to understand why the Commission in its latest Action Programme on the environment, *Towards Sustainability* (OJ C138 17.5.93 p1), has proposed that the effect on the environment should be a consideration whenever any kind of Community law is made.

Objectives

The objectives of the Community policy on the environment are listed in article 130r of the EC Treaty, and include the protection of health, the prudent use of natural resources, and the promotion of international measures to deal with environmental problems. It was not until 1987 that a section dealing with the environment, Title XVII, articles 130r to 130t, was added to the Treaty by the Single European Act.

A series of action plans on the environment have been approved by resolutions of the Council. Resolutions have no binding effect, but are used to make declarations, accept agreements in principle, or welcome communications from the Commission. The action plans indicate the strategy behind the laws enacted by the Community; over the last twenty years they have given rise to over 200 items of legislation. The First Action Programme (OJ 1973 C112 20.12.73 p1) introduced the principle that the polluter pays, and said that the best policy consists in preventing the creation of pollution at source. The programme comprised a list of remedial measures, and concentrated on the need for environmental protection standards to fix the levels of pollution that are to be regarded as tolerable. The Second Programme (OJ C139 13.6.77 p1) proposed that more account should be taken of the environmental aspects of planning and land use; one result of this policy was a directive on the need for environmental assessments, Council Directive (EEC) 85/337 (OJ L175 5.7.85 p40). This is implemented in the UK by the Town and Country Planning (Assessment of Environmental Effect) Regulations SI 1988/1199 as amended. The object of the directive is that development consent, for projects likely to have an effect on the environment, should be granted only after an assessment of their effect. The assessment must be conducted on the basis of information supplied by the developer and others concerned by the project. Member States must ensure that the major projects listed in Annex I, such as oil refineries and motorways, are subject to an environmental assessment, but it is left to their discretion whether the more minor projects in Annex II are subject to assessment; the United Kingdom has chosen to adopt legislation imposing environmental assessments for Annex II schemes, for example the Environmental Assessment (Salmon Farming in Marine Waters) Regulations 1988 SI 1988/1218.

The Third Programme (OJ C46 17.2.83 p1) and Fourth Programme (OJ C328 17.12.76 p1) resulted in more remedial measures, but the Fifth Programme, *Towards Sustainability*, (OJ C138 17.5.93

p1) is not intended to be merely palliative. It will last until the end of the century and is concerned to promote sustainable growth, one of the objectives set out in article B of the Union Treaty. In order to achieve this it is hoped that the consumption patterns of society will be altered so that raw materials will be recycled, waste of natural resources prevented and pollution avoided. Previous action programmes relied on purely legislative measures, but the new programme will have a broader mix of remedies, for example fiscal incentives, horizontal measures on scientific research, and improved arrangements for structural funds. The Commission hopes to secure shared responsibility at all levels in governments, local authorities and commerce for the health of the environment.

European environmental law has developed in a haphazard way, so it is difficult to ascertain any structure. There are directives on the following subjects: pollution of the atmosphere, water and soil, waste management, safeguards in relation to chemicals and biotechnology, product standards, environmental assessments, and the protection of nature. International measures also form a part of EC environmental law; conventions that have been ratified by the Community rank below primary legislation, but above secondary legislation, and thus prevail over conflicting directives. The Community has ratified a number of conventions on the environment, such as the Barcelona Convention for the Protection of the Mediterranean Sea Against Pollution (OJ 1977 L240 19.9.77 p1).

The directives

The Community sets emission and limit values for pollutants; it is helpful to understand these terms since they occur frequently in directives on the environment. For example, Council Directive (EEC) 84/360 (OJ L188 16.7.84 p20), a directive on air pollution that makes special authorization necessary for the operation of certain kinds of industrial plant, defines *air quality limit values* as the concentration of polluting substances in the air during a specified period which is not to be exceeded, and defines *emission limit values* as the concentration or mass of polluting substances that is not to be exceeded during a specified period. Another directive on air pollution, Council Directive (EEC) 85/210 (OJ L96 3.8.85 p25), sets limit values for lead in petrol.

Council Directive (EEC) 76/464 (OJ L129 18.5.76 p23) is the framework directive on the protection of water from pollution. It obliges the Council to set limit values for various dangerous substances, and applies to inland waters, territorial waters, internal coastal waters and ground water. Member States must have a system under which prior authority is required before certain dangerous substances may be discharged into water; the authorization must lay down emission standards. As to bathing water, quality is assured by Council Directive (EEC) 76/160 (OJ L31 5.2.76 p1).

Directives on noise include Council Directive (EEC) 86/594 (OJ L344 6.12.86 p24) which concerns measuring and monitoring methods, and limit values for noise from household appliances.

The framework directives on waste, Council Directives (EEC) 75/442 (OJ L194 25.7.75 p39) and 78/319 (OJ L84 31.3.78 p43), are drafted in broad terms, and oblige Member States to prevent toxic and dangerous waste, or at least ensure its safe disposal, and to take steps to encourage the recycling and reprocessing of waste, in accordance with the principle that the polluter pays.

Very green manufacturers can now obtain an award under the Community eco-label award scheme, which was created by Council Regulation (EEC) 880/92 (OJ L99 11.4.92 p1). To qualify for such an award, their product must have a reduced environmental impact during its entire life cycle, without compromising either the safety of workers or its effectiveness. Those fortunate enough to win this accolade will be able to display upon their wares a droopy EC daisy with twelve stars for petals.

Direct effect

The problem with the environmental directives is that they do not usually have any direct effect. For instance, in a case in the Scottish Court of Session, *Kincardine and Deeside District Council and others* v. *Forestry Commission* (8 March 1991 *transcript*), Coulsfield J had to decide whether the directive on environmental assessments, Council Directive (EEC) 85/337 (OJ L175 5.7.85 p40), applied to an application made to the Forestry Commission for a grant of planning permission for certain work. The Environmental Assessment (Afforestation) Regulations 1988 came into force two days after the application was made, too late for the applicant to rely upon them. Instead he tried to pray in aid the direct effect of the directive, but he was unsuccessful because the planning application related to agriculture and was therefore made under Annex II of the directive. The directive could not be read as being so precise and unconditional as to have direct effect because, in the case of those projects listed in Annex II, it was left to Member States to decide whether an environmental impact assessment had to take place or not.

There are, however, three matters that do not depend on further action by the Council or Member States, and so should generally be sufficiently precise and unconditional to have direct effect, namely, maximum or limit values and concentrations, prohibitions, and obligations to act. For example, the directive on drinking water, Directive (EEC) 80/778 (OJ L229 30.8.80 p11), states that the nitrate content of drinking water must not exceed 50 mg per litre. The United Kingdom has failed to implement this directive, as Case C–337/89 *Commission* v. *United Kingdom* (25 November 1992 *transcript*) shows. If Cases C–6/90 and C–9/90 *Frankovich* v. *Republic of Italy* and *Bonifaci* v. *Republic of Italy* [1993] 2 CMLR 66 are correctly decided (see Chapter 7 of this book) it ought to be possible to sue the State for the breach, if damage can be shown.

An example of a prohibition is to be found in Council Directive (EEC) 79/409 on the conservation of wild birds (OJ L103 25.4.79 p1). This, apart from imposing on Member States an obligation to establish a system for the protection of wild birds, also states that they shall prohibit, for certain species, the sale, transport for sale, keeping for sale and offering for sale of birds dead or alive.

An example of an obligation to act is to be found in the environmental impact assessment directive, in the obligation to carry out an environmental assessment before the grant of development consent for the projects listed in Annex 1, although, as the following case shows, attempts to use it directly in English courts have not met with success. *Twyford Parish Council and others* v. *Secretary of State for Transport* [1991] C O D 210 concerned an application under Schedule 2 of the Highways Act 1980. After twenty years of debate, between 1977 and 1988, a route was chosen for a four-lane motorway which would destroy two ancient monuments, and cut a trench of devastation through the natural beauties of Twyford Down. The plaintiffs argued that the Secretary of State was obliged to take account of the environmental assessment directive, but McCullough J held that it was not intended to apply to projects already begun, that only those who had suffered as a result of a breach had a remedy and then only against others than the State, that on the facts there was no breach of the directive, and that therefore there was no reason to refer the case to the European Court. The case antedates *Frankovich* v. *Italy* (see above) and one wonders now whether the second proposition is correct.

The complaints procedure

A cheaper and, in the long run, more effective way of implementing EC environmental law is to make a complaint to the Commission. As was explained in Chapter 6, anyone can make a complaint to the Commission about an infringement of EC law. There is a form available (OJ C26 1.2.89 p6) but there is no obligation to use this. Complaints concerning environmental law are dealt with by DG XI. Any complaint will be registered and given a file number, but if the Commission's lawyers find no apparent breach of EC law they will immediately close the file and so inform the complainant.

General grumbling, such as that the air at Prestatyn is not bracing, is not treated as a complaint. The allegations must be sufficiently particular for an investigation to be made. If there is an apparent breach the Commission sends an informal letter, usually known as an article 169 letter, to the Member State, setting out the alleged breaches and inviting a response within, usually, two months.

In 1992 there were sufficient complaints from the public about plans to build motorways through Oxleas Wood and Twyford Down for the Commission to write such a 169 letter to Malcolm Rifkind, the Secretary of State for Transport. It is unusual to publish the contents of such a letter, but his response is set out in the *Journal of Planning Law*, 92 JPL 21, and this shows that he was asked to stop the work on these projects because of an alleged failure to implement the environmental assessment directive. The reason why this particular dispute arose was that although the bulldozers had yet to do their worst, most of the planning processes had begun before the directive on environmental assessments was implemented, and the question was whether the pre-existing planning procedures had made a sufficient assessment of the impact on the environment.

The next stage in the complaints procedure is that the Commission reconsiders the case. It can conduct a further investigation, or close the file, or decide to start formal infringement proceedings. If it chooses the latter a formal notice of complaint is sent in a letter to the Member State and the complainant is informed that this has been done, although he will not be told its contents. A period of at least two months (in practice, longer) is allowed for any reply.

The Commission then considers the case again; it may still simply close the file or make further investigations. But if it is not satisfied it can send a reasoned opinion to the Member State. Once the reply has been received, or the period in which it is to be sent has expired, the Commission can bring a case against the Member State in the European Court. The procedure under Article 171 of the Treaty means that, ultimately, a Member State could be fined, but it is clear that the procedure is so prolix that this would be an unlikely event.

It is possible, however, for the Commission to make an interim decision obliging a Member State, if the case is urgent, to cease work upon some project until it can be investigated. The threat of this, in the case of Oxleas Wood, was sufficient to make the government reconsider its position, and the wood was saved from destruction.

Framework agreements

The Community rules on the environment have been resented by the United Kingdom because they are too inflexible. The imposition of limit values, in particular those for pollutants in water, at levels which cannot practicably be met has meant that the United Kingdom has been continuously criticised for failure to implement Community standards. At a European Council meeting in December 1993, however, the European leaders agreed to replace the existing drinking and bathing water directives with framework agreements which will leave most of the detailed regulation, hitherto prescribed in the directives, to national authorities.

Chapter 16

Agriculture

The Common Agricultural Policy (CAP) is best understood by those who have read *Genesis*. It will be recalled that it was Joseph who originally thought of the idea. Pharaoh, having had serious differences with the food processing industry, arrested the Head Baker and the Chief Butler. While they were on remand Joseph, their cell-mate, demonstrated a talent for the interpretation of dreams, predicting that the Chief Baker would be hanged.

The Butler, happily, was acquitted and reinstated. One day he heard that Pharaoh had a bad night dreaming about food shortages, and put in a word for Joseph. The latter, having foreseen seven years of plenty and seven years of famine, was asked to formulate a plan to deal with the problem.

Joseph proposed that commissioners should be appointed to buy up the corn of Egypt during the years of plenty. This meant that the price of grain would be maintained in times of surplus. When there were shortages Pharaoh would be able to guarantee supplies. So impressed was Pharaoh that he took up the idea, discovered that it enabled him to finance structural reforms, and bought up all the land in Egypt.

Articles 38 to 47 of the Treaty deal with the Common Agricultural Policy. Maastricht has not made any changes to these articles, save that the policy now has a more humble status; it used to be found in a part of the Treaty headed 'Foundations of the Community', but is now placed in Part Three, which is modestly headed 'Community Policies'.

Competition

Article 42 of the Treaty states that the provisions of the chapter relating to the rules on competition apply to the production and trade in agricultural products only to the extent determined by the Council. This exception is now of little practical effect. Council

170

Regulation 26 (OJ 1962 p 993, OJ Sp Edn 1959–62 p129) has brought into effect articles 85 to 90 of the Treaty in relation to agriculture. Articles 85 to 90 of the Treaty now apply to all agreements decisions and practices referred to in articles 85(1) and 86 of the Treaty which relate to production of or trade in agricultural products. Regulation 26 does not, however, include article 92 which deals with state aid.

Structure of CAP

The objectives of the Common Agricultural Policy are set out in article 39 of the Treaty:

(a) to increase agricultural productivity;
(b) to ensure a fair standard of living for the agricultural community;
(c) to stabilize markets;
(d) to assure the availability of supplies;
(e) to ensure that supplies reach consumers at reasonable prices.

In order to attain the above objectives article 40 of the Treaty requires Member States to develop a common organization of agricultural markets. The financial arrangements for this are contained in article 40(4) which, in order to enable the common organization to attain its objectives, provides for one or more agricultural guidance and guarantee funds to be set up. The European Agricultural Guidance and Guarantee Fund (EAGGF), often referred to by its French initials FEOGA, is divided into two parts: a Guidance Section which finances structural policy and a Guarantee Section concerned with expenditure relating to refunds on exports and intervention measures. The Commission is responsible for the administration of the fund.

A common organization of agricultural markets could have been achieved under article 40 by means of common rules on competition, or the compulsory co-ordination of national market organizations; in practice it has been achieved by means of a European market organization, that is to say the replacement of individual arrangements for marketing produce by a system which applies throughout the Community. This European market organization has been constructed from a series of Council Regulations. There is a regulation for each kind of product affected: Council Regulation (EEC) 1766/92 (OJ L181 1.7.92 p21) deals with cereals; Council Regulation (EEC) 804/68 (OJ L148 28.6.68 p13, Sp Edn 1968 (I) p176) deals with milk products; Council Regulation (EEC) 822/87 (OJ L84 27.3.87 p1) deals with wine; Council Regulation (EEC) 1035/72 (OJ L118 20.5.72 p1) deals with fruit and vegetables, and so on. Nearly every agricultural product has its own regulation setting out its regime. There are some twenty of these main regulations. The main Council regulations have sprouted a number of ancillary and implementing regulations.

Some regulations, for example Commission Regulation 3665/87 (OJ L351 14.12.87 p1) on export refunds, are common to all regimes and are therefore referred to as 'horizontal regulations'. The main regulations are themselves amended frequently, but there is little consolidating legislation to aid reference.

The system differs for each regime but the salient features are as follows. An intervention price is fixed at which intervention agencies in Member States are obliged to buy in products; this ensures that the farmer will receive a proper price for his crop. A threshold price is fixed above which goods can be imported from outside the Community; this protects the internal market and is achieved by means of a variable levy.

Depending on prices on world markets, it will sometimes be advantageous to encourage exports: at other times it may be necessary to discourage exports. This balance is adjusted by means of export refunds or levies.

The system involves fixing each year a target price for each product. The target price is the level which the Community wishes to rule in the wholesale market. It will thus act as a guide to producers when they plan production.

Other terms are used in the regulations. The target price may sometimes be referred to as the base price, reference price or guide price. The intervention price may also be referred to as the floor price or purchase price.

The cereal market, which has the support of this system to the full, is the archetypal market organization. By contrast the fruit and vegetable market concentrates on quality control: common standards are set for products and producers' organizations have the power to fix a withdrawal price below which they will not offer for sale products supplied by their members.

In the United Kingdom the body responsible for intervention purchases is the Intervention Board for Agriculture. This body was created by section 6 of the European Communities Act 1972. In practice its powers are usually delegated to other agencies in the industries concerned, such as the Milk Marketing Board or the Home Grown Cereals Authority.

Reform

The existence of an intervention price has encouraged farmers to produce for intervention rather than for market. Wine lakes and butter mountains have grown and increasingly complicated measures have been taken to curb overproduction. These have included various so called co-responsibility levies, schemes for turning wine into alcohol, set aside and quotas. Nevertheless, farm incomes are not increasing and the cost of the system only swells.

Therefore in June 1992 the Council adopted a variety of measures for reform. These reforms are calculated to lower intervention prices to world market price so that the income of farmers will no longer be assured by the support of prices; direct premiums will be paid to compensate them for their loss of income.

The operation of the new system can be understood by studying the new cereals regime, which began in the 1993–1994 marketing year. The three main regulations are summarized in the following paragraphs.

Council Regulation (EEC) 1766/92 (OJ L181 1.7.92 p21) is both a consolidating and a reforming measure. The preamble states that the support provided by the market organization should be reorientated in such a way that it no longer depends solely on guaranteed prices. Target, threshold and intervention prices are fixed at gradually reducing levels for an interim period of three years. A Management Committee for cereals has been created which must be consulted before detailed rules can be made by the Council or the Commission to determine standards and qualities and the intervention centres. Imports to and exports from the Community are subject to the submission of a licence. A levy is charged on imports, and there is a system of refunds on exports.

Council Regulation 1765/92 (OJ L181 1.7.92 p2) sets up the new system of support for cereal farmers, whereby they are compensated for the loss of income they will suffer because of the reduction in intervention prices. Payment is fixed by the hectare. In order to qualify the farmer has to set land aside from production, unless he is a small producer, that is to say one with less than 20 hectares.

The co-responsibility levy, which, under the old system, was meant to discourage overproduction, has now been abolished by Council Regulation 1738/92 (EEC) (OJ L180 1.7.92 p1).

The reform of the Common Agricultural Policy has not altered the basic principles upon which it is based, that is to say market unity, Community preference and financial solidarity. Market unity means that there should be a single market, which is why the wheat regime, for example, endeavours to create an integrated market with a single price structure throughout the Community. To understand what is meant by market preference the reader should refer to Case 236/84 *Malt* v. *HZA Düsseldorf* [1986] ECR 1923, a case concerning monetary compensatory amounts on imported beef, in which it was said that in its external relations there was no principle obliging the Community to accord equal treatment to non–member countries in respect of the imposition of tariffs. Financial solidarity means that the Community pays for the Common Agricultural Policy, with the effect that financial support is distributed so as to protect as many farmers as possible.

Piggies going to market

The number of cases reaching the European Court relating to agriculture is quite large, but most do not actually involve farmers. Case 83/78 *Pigs Marketing Board* v. *Redmond* [1978] ECR 2347, [1979] 1 CMLR 177 is a useful case to begin with because it explains and illustrates the relationship between Community provisions on agriculture and other areas of the Treaty, and explains the nature of common organizations of the agricultural market.

In Northern Ireland the marketing of pigs was controlled by the Pigs Marketing Board. They had a monopoly. The law compelled farmers to sell their pigs to the Board. Regulations prohibited any transport of pigs otherwise than to one of the Board's processing centres, and by a person in possession of a permit. Mr Redmond's lorry was stopped in Armagh and discovered to contain 75 pigs; there was no permit. He protested that the prosecution was contrary to the Treaty and the rules on the common organization of the market in pigs, as set out in Council Regulation (EEC) 2759/75 (OJ L282 1.11.75 p1).

The European Court said that the common organizations of the agricultural markets are based on an open market. Every producer has free access to this market which is regulated solely by the instruments provided for by those common organizations. National practices or laws which might prevent producers from taking advantage of intervention measures or any other measures regulating the market were not compatible with the principles of such organizations.

It followed from article 38 that where there was a discrepancy between the Treaty articles relating to the Common Agricultural Policy and the rules relating to the Common Market it was the former that had precedence. Once the Community had legislated for the establishment of the common organization of the market Member States could not undermine or create exceptions to it.

Milk quotas

Milk quotas can give rise to litigation, and present curious problems to conveyancers. They are a Community invention which can perhaps be described as a kind of quasi-interest in land. Land with a quota is worth more than land without a quota but the quota cannot be sold without a land transaction, except that it is possible temporarily to transfer quota to another producer. When part of a holding is sold an apportionment of quota must be made, and Community rules provide that unused quota must be added to a national reserve of quota.

The organization of the market for milk products is provided for by Council Regulation (EEC) 804/68 (OJ L148 28.6.68 p13, Sp Edn 1968 (I) p176). This regulation, which has been substantially amended, set up a system where there is a target price for milk, an intervention price for butter, skimmed milk and certain cheeses, and a guarantee threshold price for milk. In addition there is a system for export levies and refunds.

With such market protection the result was overproduction, and the chosen method of tackling the problem was to introduce a levy, payable by every milk producer, on the quantities of milk sold for direct consumption which exceed a certain reference quantity. It is this 'reference quantity' which is usually referred to as the quota. The amendment introducing this system was made by Council Regulation (EEC) 856/84 (OJ L90 1.4.84 p10) which inserted a new article 5c into the original regulation; other regulations by the Council and Commission made detailed rules for its application. Eventually the system was simplified and codified by Council Regulation 3950/92 (OJ L405 31.12.92 p1), which extended the quota for a further seven years from April 1993. Detailed rules for the application of the quota are set out in Commission Regulation 536/93 (OJ L57 20.3.93 p12).

In the United Kingdom the system is implemented by the Dairy Produce Quotas Regulations 1993 (SI 1993 No 923). The Agriculture Act 1986 contains provisions relating to compensation to tenants for loss of milk quotas where a tenancy has ended or has been assigned. Certain questions arising under this legislation are dealt with by a Dairy Produce Quota Tribunal.

The development of the system is described by the Advocate General Sir Gordon Slynn in Case 120/86 *Mulder* v. *Minister van Landbouw en Visserij* [1989] 2 CMLR 1. The case arose because Mr Mulder had given up milk farming for a period because of a Community measure designed to encourage farmers to suspend production in return for a special premium. He found, to his dismay, that when the milk quota scheme was introduced the reference year, upon which his quota depended, fell during the very period in which he had temporarily given up dairy farming. The Court ruled, however, that he had a legitimate expectation that he would receive a quota. The Council was therefore bound to protect that expectation, and the relevant measure was held to be invalid in so far as it did not allow him to receive a quota.

Mr Mulder was then able to bring an action for compensation against the Council and the Commission, and was awarded damages in a sum equivalent to the difference between what he earned and what he would have earned had he been awarded a quota: see Case C104/89 and C37/90 *Mulder* v. *EC Council and EC Commission* [1992] ECR I–3061.

Structural policy

The Common Agricultural Policy has, for the most part, directed its effort to price and market policies. There have, however, been some efforts directed towards modernization and improvements in the efficiency of farms. For example, Council Directive (EEC) 75/268 (OJ L128 19.5.75 p1) authorizes Member States to introduce a system of aid for hill farmers, and there is a Community aid scheme to encourage elderly farmers to take early retirement, made under Council Regulation (EEC) 2079/92 (OJ L215 30.7.92 p91); in each case the arrangements are partly financed by the European Agricultural Guidance and Guarantee Fund. Council Regulation (EEC) 2328/91 (OJ L218 6.8.91 p1) is a consolidating measure on improving agricultural structures. It requires member states to introduce an aid system to encourage set–aside of arable land and the conversion of production to non–surplus products. It also includes specific measures to assist farming in less favoured areas and thus augments Council Directive 75/268 (above).

Rotating pigs

The Common Agricultural Policy has given rise to absurdities such as those concerning monetary compensatory amounts. These require some explanation if the reader is to understand some of the recent reforms.

The Common Agricultural Policy means that the Community continuously fixes intervention prices and the other guide prices for agricultural produce. These prices are fixed in ECUs. No one has ever seen an ECU; it is simply an accounting device. There has to be an exchange rate by which the ECU can be converted into the national currencies of Member States. Member States have not been willing to accept the consequences for farm prices that would follow if the market rate of exchange were used. Instead, an artificial rate of exchange is used which has become known as Green Money; in the case of the United Kingdom it is, of course, the Green Pound. Since Green Money will not necessarily correspond with the market rate there may be a difference in the price of agricultural products between Member States and this must be evened out in some way.

One solution has been a system whereby so called monetary compensatory amounts (MCAs) were paid either as a levy (negative MCA) or a subsidy (positive MCA) on exports and imports. The system meant that you could, for example, collect money simply for exporting your pig. If you could find a way of getting your pig back without paying a levy you could collect your compensatory amount again. This gave rise to constantly circulating pigs a situation which brought the system into disrepute. Commission Regulation (EEC) 3137/91 (OJ L297 28.10.91 p17) laid down detailed rules for dismantling monetary compensatory amounts; the system was eliminated by 1 January 1993 because it could not survive the elimination of border controls. Council Regulation (EEC) 3813/92 (OJ L387 31.12.92 p1) substitutes new arrangments which include compensatory aid.

Bibliography

The following may be useful further reading for those in need of introductory texts:

Korah, V. *An Introductory Guide to EEC Competition Law and Practice*, ESC Publishing.

Krämer. *EEC Treaty and Environmental Protection*, Sweet and Maxwell.

Rudden and Wyatt. *Basic Community Laws*, Oxford University Press.

Steiner, J. *Textbook on EEC Law*, Blackstone Press.

Wallace, R and Stewart, W. *Butterworths Guide to the European Communities*, Butterworths.

Weiss, F. *Public Procurement Law*, Athlone Press.

Wooldridge, F. *Company Law in the United Kingdom and the European Community*, Athlone Press.

Index